Halide Edip Adivar

Sinekli Bakkal, or the Clown and his Daughter

Part I

Translated from the Turkish by W. D. Halsey

TRANSLATOR'S PREFACE

This is a translation of Part I of the Turkish version of *Sinekli Bakkal* by Halide Edip Adivar, published in 1936. She published the novel first in English under the title, *The Clown and his Daughter*, in 1935, but the translator, who began the translation in 2002 and finished it in rough form in 2007, worked exclusively from the Turkish version.

Part I

Chapter One

This narrow back street took its name from that of the neighborhood where it was found: Sinekli Bakkal, that is, grocery with flies. It was a street of wooden, two-storied houses. The roofs were dilapidated. Their old eaves stretched out, extending one to another. If there ever was a gap that remained from one peak to another, it formed but a dark vaulted passageway over the street. At sunrise and sunset, this gap became a path of light changing from color to color. But the sides of the street were always dark and chilly.

If you stood at the street corner and looked around, in every window there were flowerpots made of red earth and dark boxes. In the flowerpots were red, white, purple geraniums, fuchsias, carnations. In the boxes were heaps and heaps of green fezes. Right at the corner was a wisteria arbor, under which was the busiest fountain of the neighborhood. Behind all these was a thin, long, white minaret that resembled stage scenery.

Behind the latticed windows were strung hordes of crone-heads. When they took a break in their sewing, they gossiped at the top of their voices. On the street, with clogs on their feet, hand-painted scarves on their heads, and copper buckets in their hands, women came and went to the fountain. On stoops girls with their hair plaited in two pigtails chewed gum; barefoot boys with torn trousers and bare heads squatted down around pools of water in the middle of broken paving-stones and floated paper ships.

This place was not very different from a poor neighborhood in any part of the world. Rather than a passage-way, it was a meeting place: here neighbors kept up with their friends, chatted, fought, amused themselves. Here no phase of life was absent: the old people would laugh as they told the story of the woman who even gave birth at the fountain head.

When a stranger stops, if he strikes up a friendship with the women drawing water, a hennaed

4

finger will surely point out two places: one is the "Istanbul Grocery" of Mr. Mustafa, and the other, opening its back windows over the fountain, is the house of the Imam. The former is a shop recessed like a black hole under one of the houses in the middle of the street, the latter is the only three-storied building of the street. Although it opens its door on the street, nevertheless Sinekli Bakkal has little desire to welcome it, because rich and poor, in fact all the neighborhood people, are forced to come to the house for every one of life's occasions such as deaths, births or marriages.

Mr. Mustafa was a niggardly, a disagreeable neighborhood grocer according to the relation of every eulogist. The Imam? If anyone paid attention he was like every neighborhood Imam, but in fact he was unlike anyone other than himself.

He had two bushy eyebrows that stood up like hedgehog bristles, two small sharp gimlet-eyes that focused inward, black like charcoal and burning like hot coals. His nose was long and like a fox. His beard was black with much grey in it. He was short of stature and meager of body. But inside the large whiteness of his turban and the broad cuffs of his Ottoman overcoat his ponderous swaying walk gave him a certain majesty. He had a large, rich voice that even half-grown boys envied. He spoke with a passionate ease as if giving a sermon, even his day-to-day conversation was like someone reading the Koran, and each "alif" came out of his mouth with ornaments and flourishes.

Those who sought death certificates and marriage licenses underwent constant haggling with him that ended with their calling him a niggardly, a cheap Imam. But they still faithfully attended his sermons at the small mosque, a little fearful in his presence, or just ill at ease.

Whether or not the Sinekli Bakkal Imam belonged to the fourteenth century or to the terrible period of Abdülhamid II,[1] with the fire of his eyes, the fearfulness of his dogma, and especially the power of his manner he seemed to be one of those fanatics who herd each and every thought in order and gather herds behind them.

---

[1] Abdülhamid II ruled the Ottoman Empire from 1876 to 1909.

The dogmas by which he wanted to inspire the congregation were sharp as a knife. In life for a human being there are two roads: one to heaven, the other to hell. In his sermons, the Imam would explain that the second road is more glorious, more human. There is no nook and cranny that hell does not know, no shape that can describe its punishments. According to him, travelers on the road to hell are addicted to sensual pleasure. He explains it thus, that for a youth of his congregation at first his desire awakes him to join with these ignoramuses. The travelers on the road to heaven are an altogether different type of person. They do not laugh, they do not play, they neither take comfort nor give comfort to others. For them, pleasure and what gives merriment, all these things are sins. Every act involved in thoughts of play and diversion is a cardinal sin. Their faces are open, their hearts are full of pain, every moment is filled with thoughts of the other world. In the Imam's sermons, he never busied himself with such things as thoughts of badness and goodness and moral precepts like help for the poor, not to tell a lie, not to break a heart. Against pleasure and joy, and in general any manifestation of life, he nursed an unceasing grudge, an unpardoning enmity. Thus when he made his rounds, smiles froze on lips, laughter died, children scattered like a covey of partridges.

The Imam lost his wife young and nobody came to his house any more. There was no one but a girl named Emine. She was a little girl of a white taut complexion, pink-cheeked, with thin lips that snapped shut like a mouse-trap and small black eyes. She was clean, industrious, fastidious, and did not condescend to play with the neighborhood children. Sour-faced, without laughter, she seemed a solitary symbol of the Imam's creed. But, contrary to what people expected, it was by her hand that unlucky chance delivered a most bitter blow to the Imam. When the girl was seventeen years old, she ran away with a youth, famous for laziness in the neighborhood, who was nicknamed "girl Tevfik" because he played the role of the "zenne"[2]. Fundamentally their relations began in the arrangement of rows in the school-

---

[2] In the orta oyunu, a traditional Turkish drama similar to commedia dell'arte, with improvised rather than written dialogue, and with stock characters, among whom is the "zenne", the female character, played by Tevfik. Orta oyunu means literally play in the middle, and orta is sometimes given as the etymology of commedia dell'arte, the Italians having Italianized orta incorrectly to arte.

house. The two children squeezed their knees together in front of the same reading-desk, they followed the same assistant master to the school and as the rows started to recite they said the prayer "by the rivers of paradise" from one mouth. And thus these two children, who resembled one another neither outwardly nor inwardly, were united by habit with a mysterious force that came from neither mathematics nor logic.

As for Tevfik, at that time he was long legged, sturdy, his chestnut colored eyes were sweet like a girl's, his red lips were continually talking, he was a mischievous boy, a cut-up.

He had amused the whole neighborhood by imitating everyone from the moment he began to walk and talk.

He went to bed and rose in the house of the grocer Mr. Mustafa, the brother of Tevfik's widowed mother. In spite of every insistence of the old man, he neither became an apprentice anywhere, nor did he learn a craft. At loose ends, he never stopped haunting the streets of Istanbul. Nevertheless, along with all his flightiness, he exhibited the traits of the artistic types that Istanbul grows like weeds.

Very early on he began to be famous as an artist when he put on the play of Karagöz on evenings during Ramadan in his uncle's garden. Mr. Mustafa had no objection when he saw that the boy got pocket change from this work. As soon as he received a permission that he obtained more easily than he thought, Tevfik put on his shoulder old cardboard boxes from the attic, brought them downstairs; snitched five or ten colored pens from the shop, and for one whole week he sliced, cut, painted; he put forth a procession of paper art. He even added one of two new characters to the cast of Karagöz.

The principal of those were a grocer who resembled Mr. Mustafa and, resembling the Imam, a large squat old turbaned imam. And a little neighborhood beauty who was the twin of Emine. For a week of evenings, as "image and shadow" appeared, Tevfik set up the curtain, lit the candle, and appeared as a procession of elderly men among the child spectators. He earned such popularity in the neighborhood that on one evening of that week he played only to women. When the caricatures of the Grocer and the Imam appeared at the curtain, among the grown-ups a light whisper started; as soon as the neighborhood cutie appeared, the kids were stamping their feet, they struck up a tune, chanting "It's Emine, Emine."

At nineteen years, Tevfik became one of the most famous players of the woman's role in the "orta oyunu". As for the play "Çirpici Çayiri" they went to the show to see what their neighbor would do.

The men did not give him the cold shoulder. Nevertheless, it touched on their honor, the mincing gender of a young man who had grown up in their neighborhood, who put a charcoal mole on his face, penciled his eyebrows, put on eye-shadow. But even the most serious broke apart from laughter at his clowning. Even the Minister of Justice Selim Pasha, whose mansion was on the well-bred side of the district, came to see Tevfik, and let forth a ha-ha-ha with a lightness that hardly befitted his reputation.

The same year, following one suddenly upon the other, came the loss of Tevfik's uncle and his mother. On one hand, the shop, the house and the vegetable garden behind it remained; on the other hand, a type of emptiness and sadness took its place and filled his heart. These two events, for one reason or another, fanned the flames of the relationship between Emine and Tevfik that continued essentially unchanged behind the cage, from their doorways. The Istanbul Grocery was a busy shop, a grocer who knew his business would be able to earn excellent money there. This was much on Emine's mind. Anyhow, her eye was on Tevfik. Like all dominating natures, she discerned in Tevfik, molded like wax in her matrix, an ideal husband. As soon as she had a promise from the mouth of Tevfik that he would leave his playing and work as a grocer, she ran away from the house of the Imam. The neighborhood helped the young people in order to tweak the nose of the Imam. Their marriage was performed in another neighborhood. The day that his daughter came to Tevfik's house, in the presence of the neighborhood the imam repudiated Emine.

Chapter Two

The Imam's daughter that he had waited for at street corners was one person, and the wife of Tevfik the grocer was quite another Emine. Tevfik found this out quite soon. The thin pink lips that caused his heart to beat violently now became an unpleasant mouth that raised nagging and grumbling to a high art-form... In place of the heat of black eyes that dissolved Tevfik's blood in his veins, now rather more in those eyes appeared malicious glints and cold ice. For the sake of this woman, had he entered a trade that, compared to acting, was nothing else but slavery? In spite of everything, if he had not still been so powerfully in love with this woman, he would have certainly taken a decision to return to playing in the orta oyunu.

Whatever you do, she is picky, bad-tempered, but still she dominates Tevfik; her heart is vain, her head is narrow, her tongue is poison, but Tevfik has not yet had his fill of her. When Tevfik added up the balance-sheet of his married life, he stops when he comes to this point. And being a grocer is not all that bad. Especially when Tevfik saw there were very comic sides to it so that he could do it as he himself wished.

The curses of Emine were much more bitter than those of Tevfik. Very soon she began to recall the house of her father with longing. Although Tevfik had not changed very much, Emine's addiction to him began to wane. His wittiness that was welcome from a distance, his rowdiness never ceasing for a minute to pester Emine ... she became a little tired of these things. Especially when she compared Tevfik to her father, she thought him much inferior. The Imam was clean, he was orderly, he got up early, he made almost no small talk at home. Worship and earning money ... all his time, all his effort was devoted to these two occupations.

But Tevfik?

First of all, he was dirty. Moreover, it was not clear when he ate, got up, or worked. It was necessary to pull him by the leg to get him out of bed in the morning. By smoking in bed, he smeared the bed sheets with ash, and made Emine blow her stack.

After getting up, he wanted one thing after another from Emine, and the woman had no patience for him.

If at least he had been skillful at his work ... The shop was a jumble, the merchandise was off-date, polite customers were leaving one by one and every day the riff-raff increased. He was continually giving credit and customers who promised to pay at the beginning of the month were causing trouble for Tevfik. And as if that was not enough, the theatrical friends with whom he had sworn to break off relations were continually hanging off his neck, asking for loans of money. Anyhow, if Tevfik stayed for five minutes in his shop, he would fly out to the street, slide down, and would play the "steel stick" among the children.

Very often he would do an imitation of a cat, dog, rooster or chicken for them, and a procession of men would congregate in front of the shop, a revelry would ensue. In short, Tevfik turned the grocery shop, even the street, into a fairground.

The thing that made Emine madder than any of these things was that someone saying "money" in the skull of her husband would not have had any value. Thus if beggars come and speak to her husband, he immediately saying "alms for those who have passed on" becomes a blind beggar making his rounds on Friday evening; if perchance his wife points out her father to him as an example he immediately sucks in his chin, alters his voice, and in the most unctuous manner of the Imam starts haggling over a death certificate with an imaginary woman.

At last Emine spoke her final word. If Tevfik did not improve, she would put herself at the head of the counter and be the grocer and she would use him as an apprentice. And one day she put the yeldirme[3] on her back, the head-scarf on her head, and she moved to the head of the counter.

Before long, under the administration of Emine, the shop began to function better than in the days of Mr. Mustafa. From now on, the shop was clean inside and out, the goods were each in its proper place, goods were produced for each customer according to his wishes, the word spread out to every customer. She quickly increased the number of cash customers and avoided the trouble of credit. Nobody came to the shop anymore just to run his jaw.

Emine began to have a little peace. Fundamentally she had so much work that she couldn't find time to argue with Tevfik. She now used him only in the work that she had not done, in his own house and shop, as an apprentice, as a foster-child to feed and keep around.

Emine's behavior, which gravely wounded Tevfik's feelings, did not make for a new atmosphere in the shop. The cash customers of Emine got on his jangled nerves. As soon as someone wearing clean clothes entered the shop, she made such a change that ... her frowning face was soon smiling, her narrowed lips opened up. She was constantly giving orders to Tevfik.

Tevfik's indigent customers now entered the shop like convicts into prison walls and Emine did not let escape any opportunity to boil those who had contracted debt.

As Tevfik began to perceive himself a stranger in his own shop, he very frequently would disappear. He no longer responded to Emine's reprimands with clowning; he would crouch down in a corner and think. And meanwhile he would scan Emine intently.

This peace, this submission did not satisfy Emine very much; suspicion began to enter inside her. She had sensed that there was a closed side to this open man whom she had considered her entire property. To learn what he did when he was in the street, what he thought when he

---

[3] The outer dress worn by Turkish women.

was in the house, she applied every trick: nagging, sweet talking, fighting ...but she was not successful. Thank God every day she was so tired from working that as soon as she had said the yatsi prayer, she went upstairs and to bed.

Late one night, Emine was suddenly woken by the sound of voices coming from below, she sat up straight in her bed. Tevfik's place a moment ago by her side was empty. She took her slippers in her hand, and slowly slowly started down the stairs. The door from the landing to the shop was half open, inside a lamp was burning. She fit her face to the gap, she made an inspection of the shop.

In the yellow light of gas lamps, she saw a layer of cigar smoke blanketing the air. Men of wondrous shapes were smoking cigars as they sat on sugar and soap boxes. The major part of these were ne'er-do-well friends of Tevfik that she herself had driven away from the shop. There was a dwarf whom she didn't know, wearing a yellow smock and a white cotton turban embroidered with yellow silk, sitting cross-legged on a wooden bench. In any event, they were all very merry, clapping their hands and laughing. They had fixed their eyes on the middle of the shop as if watching a strange event.

Emine soon learned what the "strange event" was. Tevfik was making an imitation of Emine. On his back was a woven blanket for a yeldirme, a sugar sack on his front for an apron, a napkin on his head for a head-scarf ... But the strangest part of the imitation was not his dress. Tevfik had narrowed his broad face, shrunk his large sweet eyes until they were sharp needles, until they became two small gimlet-eyes. With a thin and whistly voice he was haggling over dried beans. However, he altered this voice very frequently according to the imaginary customer who entered the shop. And their eyes never left Tevfik.

As the scene in the shop came to an end, Tevfik began to imitate the situation in Emine's bedroom. Holding up a tin box that was on top of the counter to his face as a mirror, puffing out his upper lip with his tongue, he plucked out his upper lip hair with an imaginary tweezers. This was a direct violation of his intimacy with a woman. What Moslem would have been capable of exposing his lawful spouse in this way?

A human whirl-wind on the landing was the result. The kitchen door gap opening to the house struck the dwarf like a thunderbolt. A hoarse female voice: screamed "Blabbermouth liars, dogs of a clown!"

In front Tevfik, in back the dwarf, treading on one another's heels, fled to the street from the wrath of Emine, and suddenly vanished into blackness.

Chapter Three

Miss Ebe Zehra waited for Tevfik at the door of the Istanbul Grocery until almost noon. After the night's outrage Emine had fled to the house of the Imam and had sworn to kill herself if he did not take her in.

The old man, who knew full well the obstinacy of his daughter, when he ran into Miss Zehra in the morning, sent her to Tevfik. They were proposing an immediate divorce. And if she was divorced, Emine would never return to the shop.

Tevfik, believing that he had hurt Emine in a sensitive place and thinking about how she would forgive him, came to the shop as late as possible. When he saw the old woman with a frowning face in front of the gate, he was confused. When the women explained why she had taken her position at the shop, his confusion redoubled. In spite of every sort of trouble, life without Emine was difficult for him to imagine. However much he had the habit of vagabondage, of empty wandering, he had just as much need to be a slave of someone, somebody's property. He had not been this afraid of being alone after the loss of his mother. Miss Zehra had been Tevfik's midwife and loved him very much. She rubbed his back, consoled him, said that she would try to obtain a reconciliation with Emine, and after scattering a little hope into the young man's heart she left.

After this event the month that passed in the Emine-Tevfik relationship was a very romantic month according to Sinekli Bakkal. According to the women, it was like the story of Laila and Mecnun, and even the men were not displeased.

At first every day Tevfik sent Emine letters full of misspelled complaints, after that he began to loiter in front of her door, later still he made declarations of love in a loud voice under his wife's lattice.

When he got no result from this, he was reduced to drinking in the evenings and unburdening himself of his pain to the women at the fountain-head. The shop was always closed … he would wander staggering through the streets. In any event, Tevfik's condition led him to a habit of "general moral turpitude". They made a complaint to the neighborhood commissar.

The commissar summoned him one day to the neighborhood police station. Himself, he was religious, conservative, and a man who attended the Imam's sermons regularly. To him Tevfik was merely an unbeliever whose blood was lawful to shed, nothing else but a serpent whose head should be crushed. He gave Tevfik a thorough cudgelling since it was his first time there. But if he should see him any more at the Imam's door, or if he heard him burning his pain to the women, he would not leave a bone in his body unbroken.

Tevfik totally closed up his shop and disappeared from Sinekli Bakkal. But long after he had gone, Tevfik's reputation made the neighborhood echo. Again he returned to the female role in the Orta Oyunu. And this time he made an adaptation of the Orta Oyunu under the name "The Grocer's Apprentice." This was an adventure about a woman grocer and her husband's becoming her apprentice. All Istanbul broke up from laughing, even foreigners went to Göksu to see this play. This player was summoned not only to big mansions, but even to the Palace.

Emine received this news after she had returned to her father's house. The most disastrous side of the matter was that Emine had learned after leaving the shop that she was in a fairly advanced state of pregnancy. All Sinekli Bakkal said publicly that the wife in the play "The Grocer's Apprentice" was Emine. Rowdies would nudge one another and laugh when Emine passed through the street. Partly because of Emine's pregnancy, partly because of her anger toward Tevfik, the Iman applied to the court for a divorce.

Before the office of the judge, before the judicial committee, he left his sermonizing alone and explained in simple everyday words why Emine had left Tevfik. Has the Lord Judge ever seen a Muslim man displaying his lawful wife in all intimacy to the regard of friend and foe? God forbid .... he has not seen that.

After the trial had been heard, even though the people owed sweet hours to Tevfik, they grew angry at him under the influence of the speeches of the Imam. Tevfik was compelled to divorce Emine. But the story did not end with this; the gossip increased. "Religion, belief is going, things contrary to sharia are happening", they went before the Sultan and gave him the news. In order to calm the general anxiety, the Palace rendered a decision that Tevfik would leave Istanbul for a time. They exiled Tevfik temporarily to Galipoli.

After a year had gone by, Istanbul was happy and faithless, with time both the artist it had loved so much and the sins of the artist seemed to be forgotten. Only Sinekli Bakkal, when it saw Tevfik's daughter in Emine's arms, remembered him. They gave Tevfik's daughter the name Rabia.

16

Chapter Four

When Rabia was five years old, like all her equals in age of that period, she began to pour out the trays of ash and to wash coffee cups. At six years of age, she was a girl who saw to housework properly. She took care of everything her grandfather needed. These were things that were customary at that time in Sinekli Bakkal for every female child; however the thing that separated Rabia from the other children was that she was exposed early on to the influence of the Imam.

The other children, they were familiar at that age with how hammocks swayed on religious holidays, with puppet plays, but Rabia was just as familiar with places called Hell and Heaven. Mr Imam Hadji Ilhami[4] presented these two places to his granddaughter according to himself with all their attendant peculiarities. Hell awakened a deeper interest in her. When her grandfather was speaking of it, he would clench his teeth; the hair on his back would stand straight up. But she opened her eyes and listened. At first the Imam would animate this country of torment with a terror that left Dante in the dust, later he would say with a certainty that removed all doubt that it was the eternally predestined homeland of her father. The girl was afraid of Hell, but she did not find the description that the Imam gave of Heaven very attractive either. A meadow with a silent brook running through its middle came to life in her imagination. She would see sour faced huge turbaned Imams like her grandfather and severe faced women like her mother joining forces and saying prayers to God from morning to evening in a sleep inducing drone. Thus this small girl, whose mind's first imaginings were so harsh, dwelt in her first years in a neighborhood enclosed by walls of prohibition. Perhaps because of this she was forced to hide her childhood dreams in her head, to control even the expression of her face, that is to educate her will. In this period, her only rebellion was against her surroundings. In spite of the orders of her grandfather, who considered sewing a

[4] A name, meaning inspired by the Hadj, taken by Moslems to show they have been on the Hadj, or pilgrimage to Mecca.

doll a sin equivalent to making an image to be an imitation of nature, she sewed a cloth doll, sticking on a single red bead for the mouth, its eyes of blue beads and its long hair made of corn tassels, and concealed it. When her sin was discovered by Emine's sharp eyes, she defied her grandfather. She forgot with the passage of time the years that she had eaten a beating first last and foremost with the cane left over from Mr. Hadji Ilhami's school teaching days. But she never forgot the doll burning underneath the laundry cauldron. The yellow corn tassels shrinking and burning in the fire, the blue beads separating from the white cloth, these things made her see a real child being burned. A bitter lump in her throat, her eyes bone-dry, she hid her face in the stones of the kitchen and howled.

After this notable event, she did no mischief capable of causing her mother and grand-father to complain. Henceforth, having measured the power of those around her, she sensed her own weakness. She became so well-behaved that every mother in the neighborhood pointed her out to their daughters as an example. To defend their lives, like birds and insects that take on the colors of their surrounding, she also made her face, her manner and her voice conform to the expressions surrounding her, where no one smiled, no one amused himself.

Mr Hadji Ilhami, because of the gossip[5] over the Emine-Tevfik saga, did not send his granddaughter to the neighborhood school. He himself took in hand the first education of Rabia and at once found out that she was something else. He had never yet seen a hafiz learn by heart the prayer suras so quickly. And on the other hand, Emine had taken notice that the child, after hearing a song once, would sing it while she worked in a voice that was sweet and untrained as befitted her age. The father and his daughter pondered, consulted among each other, and decided to make the girl a hafiz. Was not the Imam famous in Istanbul for the education of hafizes?

For a time every morning Rabia would kneel down at a small reading desk in front of her grandfather, her thin hands on her knees, her big honey-colored eyes on the Imam's eyes, she would sway from one side to the other and memorize the Koran.

---

[5] Literally, burning mouth.

At first it was a little difficult for her to do such long memorizations in a language that she didn't know. But this passed quickly. The harmony of the Arabic language, the effect of makams resulting from words that it was half necessary to chant, the beat of the word on the final syllable like a fever pulse in the verse endings, these things all enraptured her and gave her a feeling of musical ecstasy. Her golden eyes spotted with green speckles were enveloped in smoke, her thin face became yellow, her lips dried up, her seamless voice going even to the heart, poured out as if from a waterfall, pours out harmony and with broad angles that fit her small body to this harmony, from side to side, forward and backward, with the regularity of a pendulum for an hour she was swaying and swaying.

When she was eleven, Tevfik's daughter performed her memorization publicly and became known as the smallest hafiz of Istanbul, but also the one with the most lovely sense of style and the most doleful and touching voice. She was invited on a big salary to say asir[6] and ilahi for big feasts and during Ramadan to give the response at Imperial mosques.

In her first Ramadan, she earned more money than the Imam earned in two years. Mr. Hadji Ilhami rubbed his hands with delight and explained everywhere with pride that the girl resembled him rather than Tevfik. And in those days Rabia also was glad. She felt an unknown artistic pleasure when she was successful from the excitement that her voice aroused and the congregation that surrounded her in the mosques.

Her first success and recognition happened in Valde Mosque and when she read the response there it attracted the attention of the wife of Selim Pasha.

---

[6] Asir or Asr, the afternoon prayer. Ilahi probably refers to any prayer time.

Chapter Five

A mistress of philanthropy, charitable and affectionate, her left hand was not aware of what the right had given -- this was the way Miss Sabiha, the wife of Selim Pasha, appeared from the front. But she had another side that gave rise to gossip. Addicted to the saz[7] and the human voice, she collected to herself a tribe of parasites, and would tire of them as quick as lightning, she was a woman who didn't stay on one branch! The gossip came most often from the parasites she had acquired and dumped. But not one of these affected Miss Sabiha. Her continual peals of laughter, like microbes of joy, infected all who surrounded her.

She was a friend to every person who pleased her, whether or not his age and social standing was the same as hers. Whatever time of day it was, her friends came to the mansion and plunged into her room. Along with this, if people didn't agree with her disposition, even if they were wives of ministers, she treated them very coldly. But she was still polite and with good breeding. Being very strictly of her time, she obeyed social protocol.

Emine and her daughter Rabia were not friends of Miss Sabiha and the only time that they came to the mansion was when they were among those who came to kiss her skirt on festival days and the holidays when the minarets were lit. The woman was not pleased with Emine. But it was not because her temperament was unlike the sour-faced cold daughter of the Imam ... strange to say, it was Tevfik that caused this coldness. One day when Miss Sabiha had just come to the mansion as a bride, she made his acquaintance when he was one of the neighborhood children and she had found his masquerades delightful. Usually, her carriage would stop and she would summon the boy, make him recite and thrust a shiny quarter into his hand. When Tevfik appeared in the orta oyunu, the wife of Selim Pasha became one of those who came to the show most frequently. The saga of the youth and the Imam's daughter and its sequel she had followed with attention. When Tevfik was driven into exile, she had made a request to her Pasha to keep him in his place. But Selim Pasha was not one of those

---

[7] The saz is a musical instrument, a plucked string instrument similar to a lute or the Greek bazouki.

men of importance who neglect their duty because of the opinion of a woman. Tevfik went, and Miss Sabiha's passion for the theater was finished.

The times when Mistress saw Rabia in the Valde Mosque was a critical period of her life. In the beginning her husband had been everything to her, but from now on "the time that had gone by" was a hint to devote her time to worship, or, to speak more directly, "the hour that had been stolen" was a hint to think on the other world. However the more her wrinkled face wrinkled up, she did not love thoughts of the other world. Of the worm, the scorpion, the loose, humid, black and cold earth ... But if perchance her spirit should go to heaven? That also was not a very pleasant place. In any event, the saz, the voice, jokes and mockery are forbidden there ...

She felt only fear faced with a creation that knew nothing of jokes, that never laughed and never made one laugh. Perhaps for this reason she began to attend the Mevlevi dervishes.

Besides the fact that their sheiks were jokesters, they also told her, as an explanation for the weakness of mortals, that there was a loving and pardoning Creator. Among them she became especially acquainted with a musician by the name of Vehbi Dede and she found him congenial. Vehbi Dede looked at the divine universe with a loving and understanding smile, and saw life as a divine joke. Miss Sabiha hired him at first as a music teacher for the concubines and for her step daughter Mihri. So that he might be a man who lived modestly, saying little and fasting much, Dede hardly spoke to her. With her practical head she knew that applying the softness of Dede in the mansion was capable of spoiling the well-ordered running of the house. It suited her interests to indulge the religious beliefs of Dede, but she knew she would not live his ascetic life-style.

As much as she loved folk-songs and theatrical airs, she loved serious religious music the most and this old woman was overwhelmed by Rabia's voice and manner. She was a little astonished that she was Emine's daughter. Was this the cowardly child who, upon entering her room during the festivals, crouched behind Emine? Certainly the girl must have an artistic aptitude like her father. In this beautiful voice, there was something that gave an emotion of sadness and loneliness, that put the inside of man into so much confusion. Suddenly the old woman in the condition of the small girl sensed a wretch deprived of play and joy, and this condition touched her inside. At once she made her decision. In the evening at table she said to Selim Pasha:

"Today in Valde Mosque I heard the granddaughter of the Imam. I have not heard such a response for thirty years. Send the news to the Imam, let the girl come in the evenings and recite to me a little. But for god's sake keep that worm of a mother from tagging along behind her!"

....

Skipping over the broken paving-stones of Sinekli Bakkal, Rabia followed the lantern carried by Shevket Aya, and when she came to the broad street of Selim Pasha's mansion she was overjoyed as if she had discovered a new world. Its two sides were enclosed by big gardens, in the middle of the garden there were mansions, over every gate a great big lantern ... she followed the boy through one of the gates. The scents of acacia, jasmine and honeysuckle, the plashing of the fountain ... these things gave the heart of the child a sweet beating.

The bailiff's wife was waiting in the reception room. Rabia followed her up the stairs, holding on to the double banister. In her small head, she tried to conjure into life the image of an old woman summoning her. Why had they summoned her here? She remembered the heavy leather volume that her mother had squeezed down into her armpit, the reason of this unexpected invitation. She was to read the Koran, and perhaps to recite the Ilahi. If she wondered why, there was a religious pretext for her coming to this wondrous mansion. But the air around her was in no wise the air of "the other world" ...

On the first floor their soft foot-steps sank deeply into the carpets. In long mirrors, in which chandeliers hanging from the ceiling like bunches of fruit made of light were reflected, appeared and vanished row upon row of Rabias. Behind a door, a tambourine was being played, finger cymbals tinkled, foot-steps skipped. What was the relationship of these things with the Life of Muhammad or the Koran?

She came to herself as if waking from a dream in the middle of Miss Sabiha's room. With hesitant and bashful eyes she looked at an old woman stretched out on a cushion. And the latter, with a soft blanket over her knees and pillows under her back, was giving her the once over from the place where she was. From near by there was nothing arrogant nor fearful about her. Chin on top of chin, flabby folds of skin, a wrinkled face, she had put on rouge or covering gel here and there in the middle of the wrinkles. The child found this kind of toilette a little strange. But this strange face had friendly, smiling eyes that gave her confidence. She stretched out a white hand with an emerald ring for Rabia to kiss.

"Put your book on the console and come sit here."

With her beringed hand she pointed to a place on the back-less divan. "What is your name?"

"Your slave is called Rabia."

"But you have done ... do they not call you 'big sister' Rabia?"

The young eyes of the old woman laughed sweetly, sweetly.

The mosque doormen, the neighborhood rowdies pulling the hair of the other girls, even the people who sold things in the gate, half mockingly, half tenderly, they all called her "big sister". From where had Miss Sabiha learned this? She did not laugh. She remembered she had not lifted her dress when she sat down. In her memory Emine's voice was saying: "Are you creasing your good dress again?" As if she had committed an offence, she stood up and carefully raised her dress which had been made out of the scraps of a blue pair of overalls of

23

her mother, and sat down again.

"What a stiff, thick dress this is, sister Rabia! Like a turtle shell . . ."

Rabia was of that opinion, but she was not able to laugh. She explained in an earnest voice
that her dresses were made by cutting up the cast-offs of her mother and grandfather.
Afterwards she repeated one of the speeches against finery that she had heard from the Imam.
Her eyes on the flower of the rug, she said:

"Our Lord the Prophet's clothes were patched."

A joyous peal of laughter . . . "Does Mr. Imam talk in the house just like he sermonizes?"

That a person should come and speak so lightly of her grandfather . . . when after a pause she
lifted her eyes from the flowers of the rug, she was exposed to a more wondrous question:

"At home, don't they ever talk about your father, Rabia?"

I wonder was she putting your mouth to the test? Would it divulge and teach the secret
affection of your heart for your father? She gulped, and repeated in a colorless voice the
answer the Imam had taught her to give from memory to questions about her father:

"My father is a bad man, mistress, he has never gone to the mosque ... When he dies ... he will
go to Hell."
"Not bad, he will make the demons of Hell laugh."

The mocking eyes of the woman, shining with joy and ridicule, became cloudy and stared off
into the distance. A momentary sadness at her weakness came to Rabia as her interest in her
father was aroused. She asked a question that she had hitherto not dared to ask but which
gnawed at her like a worm:

"Mistress, if my father dies, will he really go to Hell?"

"My child, if one goes to Hell, one's own loss will not touch anyone, because . . . But it is unknown, human reason does not attain to the wisdom of God, at this age that I have come to, I am no more capable of understanding what he has asked of us."

She was silent. Then she added in a voice that was half bitter half mocking:

"What Satan wants is as plain as the nose on your face, everyone's intellect attains to that as if it were water."

In any case, this topic was spoiling the customary joie-de-vivre of the old woman. Immediately she jumped to another subject. She straightened herself as she massaged her rheumatic knees with her hands. She began to talk about Tevfik's childhood. She described how sweet his street masquerades were, his Göksu plays.

When the bailiff's wife entered, Miss Sabiha quite forgot about the Imam's granddaughter with whom she had a little earlier been so occupied: each evening she administered the mansion relying on the information brought by the bailiff's wife like a commander awaiting the report of his general staff. She was almost totally chained to her room by a chronic rheumatism. Domineering and inquisitive, she would not rest until she had learned what every individual under her command did and thought. This evening she asked the bailiff's wife a mass of questions that Rabia did not understand, and the goodwife's answers were just as incomprehensible to Rabia.

"This evening what is the bearded one doing?"

"He is carving wood again; I heard the sound of the saw from the antechamber."

25

"There is no playing?"

"I heard some such thing as Miss Dürnev passed through the door. Kanarya is there also. Intellect, mistress, does not reach to the behaviors of these youths because . . ."

The bailiff's wife raised her eyes to the ceiling. She was taking shelter in God from the sins of youths named Dürnev and Kanarya. But Miss Sahiba jumped to another subject.

"What of the mustachioed worlds?"

"He is in the harem again in the piano room with the two little Beys. They are being treated to coffee after coffee."

"Did you listen?"

"How could I not listen? I glued my ear to the door for half an hour. My neck got stiff. But if I could explain anything, I would be an Arab."

"Were they speaking about women?"

"Noooope."

"It must have been politics. There was palace chatter of this and that?"

"Oh my goodness, from his mouth that talk would take wings! Does our little master talk that type of talk?"

. . . . .

The bearded one was Selim Pasha. His duty in the position of Minister of Justice of a tyrannical monarch was both difficult and delicate. In his free time, he made back scratchers from sandalwood, end tables and coffee tables. The back scratchers were especially elegant. Outwardly he had no particular passion. The people who hated the picture of Selim Pasha found nothing peculiar in its engraving that would have proclaimed his manner of gaining his living.

He was a good pater familias, and was especially devoted to his wife. Out of more than thirty years of living together, there was only one bitter fact that his wife couldn't forgive. And this too she could ascribe to many reasonable causes.

The Pasha, like every man who believes in his own greatness, had wanted a male heir who resembled himself. But the one whom Miss Sabiha called "mustachioed", her only son, in no way resembled his father. It is true that Hilmi was a well-behaved and innocuous child. The boy was gaunt, frail, addicted to music from his childhood, and he lisped.

These last two peculiarities particularly grated on Selim Pasha. After ten years of married life, when Miss Sabiha had not given birth to another child, the pasha took another wife in secret, the daughter of a wheat merchant, and installed his young wife in a neighborhood far from the mansion. The first thing his second wife did was to give birth to a girl who was more frail than Hilmi, and, two years later, she, in bearing another girl who was still-born, herself gave up her soul on the mattress of child-birth.

You can see that after this event Selim Pasha learned just how indifferent and spoiled Miss Sabiha's character was. Rather than being a woman with the courage to pour out her innermost feelings, she told him that she had been informed of his marriage, she even knew the house where she lived and indeed the name of the child. She proposed to take to her side Mihri, who was alone and motherless, and to bring her up herself as her own child. The Pasha perhaps did not guess how great a wound to her self-esteem it was, what bitter damage to her heart it did, to have a co-wife. But the thing that entranced him was that a woman was capable of hiding a secret for two years. Reticence, in his opinion, was a virtue rarely seen even in men, and in women was all the more a fantasy.

He took a decision, and moreover it was in accordance with the wishes of his heart, that he would no longer take other wives, even for the sake of procuring a male child, and at the same time his position relative to his wife changed. Now it came to pass that he listened to her thoughts with consideration and he even sometimes consulted her. If perchance a man in the Parliament should say that women were blabbermouths, he would shake his head and laugh.

With the exception of this event that was flowing into the past, there was not one single thing that she objected to in her relationship with her husband and in her home life. Meanwhile, the thing that saddened, worried her, was the different way that her son Hilmi and her husband Selim Pasha thought... The Pasha was completely a man of the old school ... Sincere and honorable according to his standards. He recognized the Sultinate as divine justice and those opposing the Sultan -- be they whosoever they may -- he thought that the responsibility of the Minister of Justice was to crush them like scorpions. There was a thing that tried him severely: the chatter of the "Young Turks". The evening when he was most joyous was certainly the evening of the day when he had a Young Turk cudgelled, had him tortured, and putting him on a steamship had him sent into exile. How many times he said: "If I see that Hilmi is a Young Turk, I will wear out his soles with the bastinado putting him to the torture, and exile him to Fizan.[8] Whereas on one hand Hilmi would read strange things to his mother, and talked about the Young Turks, even maligned the Sultan; moreover, his friends were very strange, and very much young toffs, whose hair is long, who speak French and other European tongues ... All these things, although Miss Sabiha said they were temporary manifestations of youth, as soon as she saw them again a worm dropped inside her. Oh God, if Hilmi did some imprudence, if a misfortune came upon his head? The Pasha was no protection; on the contrary, he would crush Hilmi more excessively just because he was his son. At the same time, Miss Sabiha, not liking to worry her mind with thoughts of troubles, quickly forgot this secret anxiety, and under the protection of her administration the mansion

---

[8] A province in Libya.

persevered and continued in its old regular and happy life.

At the time when Rabia came to the mansion, Miss Sabiha had yet another anxiety: there was an ongoing struggle with her daughter-in-law Dürnev and on which side victory would stay was anybody's guess. Miss Sabiha had taken Dürnev when she was small, taught her manners, given her a good education, and married her off to her son. In her hope that the young Circassian would always be bound to her and would remain in second place, she had preferred to take a daughter-in-law from a foreign country. In truth, in the days when she herself was seen and seeing in all the corners of the mansion, the voice of her daughter-in-law was not audible. But rheumatism had chained her to her corner cushion, the matter had changed, the young woman without asking her had made bold to give orders left and right.

Miss Sabiha thought of an effective way to make her limits known to her daughter-in-law. She bought a beautiful blond Circassian girl named Kanarya. Ostensibly dancing lessons were given to the girl and she said that she would give her as a gift to one of the wives of Abdülhamid. In truth this girl was to be nothing else but a threat to her daughter-in-law. However, at once Dürnev counter-attacked from a direction that the old woman did not expect. She became a bosom friend of Kanarya, she took an interest in her music and playing lessons and she began to invite her father-in-law continuously to her room, begging him to trouble himself and to indulge her by inspecting the playing and manners
of the girl who was to go to the Palace.

When Miss Sabiha said to Selim Pasha that it hardly became him to occupy himself with the playing and clothes of a young concubine, he would say with a most serious air:

"It is I who am charged with assuring the safety and well-being of the Sultan, I am compelled to investigate every person who intends to enter the Palace."

Thus you see that when the two old women were chatting about the utterly confused internal workings of the mansion, they completely forgot that Rabia was there.

Finally the bailiff said to his wife, Miss Shükriye: "The time is pretty late, take the child back…" Miss Sabiha caressed Rabia's back:

"Saturday evening is Mevlit kandil[9], I will have guests, come in the evening and you will read the Koran. Let me advise you to eat first," she said. Later on the child heard from behind her:

"Tell your mother that she can come too, after the yatsi[10] prayer."

---

[9] The evening of the prophet's birth.
[10] The midnight prayer.

Chapter 6

Dressed in a long skirt and a silk kirtle[11], her hair netted in back, her diamonds on, having even snuggled under her arm the sash of the charitable order of shefkat nishan, it was with difficulty that leaning on her cane she rose as gracious as any queen to accept the congratulations of those who came forward . . .   Rabia shrank against the sofa cushions behind her arm, with difficulty believing that this imposing lady had been the informal and friendly old woman of two days before.

First Miss Sabiha's stepdaughter, a colorless faded girl of sixteen years old, then the people of the house came forward one by one. Each one in turn said "Many happy returns!" and withdrew. However, the congratulation ceremony did not last more than ten minutes, the house people, all behind the bailiff's wife, passed and went. One alone among them Miss Sabiha detained.

At once Rabia fixed her eyes on this girl . . .   She was tall of stature, broad-shouldered, narrow hipped like a boy,   her complexion was soft and white like silk, her eyes were like two big blue enamel flowers . . . on her back was a simple pink loose kirtle, around her waist was a silver belt. Alone among the concubines, she had not tied up her head. She had plaited her yellow hair in a single plait, tied up the end with a pink ribbon, and let it dangle down her back. Rabia's mouth almost opened from amazement, watching this lovely creature. But the thing that most caught her eye was the brown eyelashes, which were slanted and upturned, and higher on one side than on the other. Why were they higher on one side than on the other? Rabia did not yet know that this was something peculiar to certain Circassians. This girl was Kanarya.

---

[11] The standard formal woman's outerdress, entari in Turkish.

Miss Sabiha asked:

"Where is Dürnev?"

"She is coming, mistress!"

And Miss Dürnev came. A small and thin young woman ... she lifted up her eyelids constantly to give a childlike glance to her huge chestnut-colored eyes. Black eyebrows plucked with care like two thin crescent moons ...   There was rouge, kohl in their proper places, on her small face an open expression. A necklace, bracelet, long earrings, rings, all were emerald. And her clothes were green velvet to match the jewels, furbellow on top of furbellow ... She was wearing a long skirt and very high heels, made of green satin ...   Once or twice one of these shoes gave a slight kick to her long skirt and all its pleats with their furbellows coiled like a snake. Rabia had to admit that she had never in her life seen a person dressed so ornately, so complexly and grandly.

Dürnev, as if in spite of the magnificence of her toilette the news that it was the eve of Kandil had not reached her, gave not a single congratulation to her mother-in-law. After saying, with a quite indifferent and formal manner, "God be praised, how healthy your color is today." she stopped under the chandelier as if involuntarily a thought had burst upon her. Whatever her thought was, the still young woman making her eyebrows play like a dancer, making her skirt ripple, the absent minded expression of her face copied from some illustrated romance, all these things grated upon Miss Sabiha's nerves.

She muttered to herself: "Disrespectful, concubine, upstart against your elder!" But nevertheless with great calm she said:

"Do you want to ask me something, my child?"

The plucked eyebrows rose, and a secret sarcasm was in her voice:

"How did you know, mistress? I was going to ask something concerning Kanarya. Does not the party of Mylady our Mistress take place in the coming week?"

"Yes."

"This evening we will have the rehearsal of Kanarya's playing. Can the Pasha come to my room even if you won't? I will play the piano."

"This evening you said?" "Yes, tonight. After yatsi."

"This is truly ridiculous! Hearing you, I can't believe that you are a Muslim girl! Have you forgotten Kandil? All the neighbors have been invited, the girl hafiz will read the Koran ..."

"What girl hafiz?"

Again opening her chestnut eyes like a child she scanned the girl in the sofa cushion, then said:

"My apartment is on the far end of the mansion, I do not see any obstacle to our having the rehearsal."

"I need Kanarya, first to show hospitality to the guests, and afterwards she will be massaging my knee."

Miss Sabiha was using her energy not to appear angry. Today she had fasted, she had performed the supererogatory prayer, she had decided to repair the last act she had done to prick her daughter-in-law. However, there is a limit to every act of patience, and Miss Sabiha had crossed by far the boundary of her patience.

Dürnev continued, still looking indifferently at the chandelier: "Is there no other concubine that can massage your knee? Nazikter does this task better. And what need is there to make such a bother that a child will read the Koran?"

"Whether one is a child or grown-up, one must read the Koran for the spirits of the dead."

The young woman responded by shrugging one shoulder to show that she had no relationship with the spirits of the dead. Her mother-in-law's face turned a deep purple under the thick layer of smoothing gel.

"In Circassian villages, there must be no hafiz so-and-so . . . your ancestors need mercy more than mine …"

Miss Sabiha stopped talking abruptly, she had said a little too much to explain from where she had come to the Kaaba. But she saw with great joy the green skirt writhing again like a viper ready to strike. The feigned child-like innocence in the eyes of the young woman vanished, her face became confused. As she opened her mouth to answer, the bailiff's wife said from the door:

"Master Pasha is coming."

The snake paused, but the air of the room remained very electric.

They saw the very tall figure of a uniformed man coming into the room. Rabia lifted her head so as to be able to see well. Because very little grey had crept into his two black drooping mustaches and his beard, Selim Pasha appeared much younger than his wife. The deep line between his thick furred eyebrows expressed the power of the master rather than age. His eyes were blue-hazel, his nose was long, its upper part regular but the lower part hooking directly at his face gave the majesty of an eagle. This face appeared sometimes harsh and severe, but also sometimes gentle, friendly, even refined. This evening it was suffused with a gentle and friendly expression.

His wife stood up leaning on her cane, the wife and her husband gave each other the Kandil greeting. But he did not see the place of his wife or the motion she made toward the small girl. His eyes did not part from his daughter-in-law. His daughter-in-law, having had one of her toys snatched from her hand, was like a sulky child. Pasha welcomed her: "How is my beautiful girl?"

Miss Sabiha answered:

"Our beautiful girl is making decisions without consulting the calendar, without conferring with us she undertakes to arrange a party on Kandil eve …"

Dürnev's eyes were on the Pasha, but her mouth said to her mother-in-law:

"Voices in my room will not come here and even supposing that they do, what harm can it cause? Do I not know your guests? They are a bunch of deaf old crones … Even inside the room they may or may not hear the voice of the child." While she was speaking, she drew near to the Pasha, her little hands stroking the gilt of his uniform, and whined in a petulant voice:

"But you will come, my lambkin Daddy Pasha …"

"Alright, alright, that is if the Mistress gives her permission…"

"Of course if you see fit …"

The victory of the daughter-in-law gave back her self control, and particularly her sobriety, to Miss Sabiha. She turned to Kanarya:

"Show Rabia downstairs, let her eat with you."

She had decided to tell her daughter-in-law to take the Imam's grand-daughter to table. But now this was not possible.

The Pasha, after everyone had left, stayed for a little while in his wife's room. Because he had guessed the effect that the gleam of triumph in Dürnev's eyes had made on his wife, he wished to counteract it a little bit.

"So your little hafiz will read the Koran to your guests ...   Whose intellect determined that the daughter of that mountebank would come here?"

"Where is Tevfik now, Pasha?"

"Since he was not a political criminal, I placed no great importance on his fate. He will still be in Gallipoli."

"I wonder if you will bring him back?" The Pasha's voice at once became firm:

"He was exiled by decree," he said, then continued more gently: "If I brought Tevfik back, the Imam would no longer send your little hafiz to us."

Miss Sabiha rose leaning on her cane:

"Let me take my abdest[12] before the guests come."

Selim Pasha remained in the doorframe, he sought his wife's eyes with his own: "It is time for bed, let me smoke a cigarette next door, Madame."

.....

---

[12] The ritual ablution before prayer.

The old women were arranged in rows on divans all around the room. On their heads were white prayer cloths, their wrinkled faces intent, their eyes with an inner ecstasy ... In their hands, multi-colored prayer beads, their fingers moving, their lips stirring as they breathed, swaying ever-so-slightly from side to side.

The viscous doleful voice of the girl hafiz made the mansion resound. Her reciting was in the perfect classical Arab style. Every note, no matter how long, was connected to its neighbor with a perfect legato. Her voice was produced through the nose in perfect rhythm, but how in command of her art was her voice and how personal her sense of style!

All the people of the mansion one by one came into the ante-room, accumulating behind the door. Among them was Selim Pasha, even the Europeanized Hilmi was there.

After the guests had dispersed and Rabia went home with her mother, Miss Sabiha stretched out exhausted on her divan and began to have Nazikter massage her knees. Much later Selim Pasha, wearing a damask cardigan and a white night cap, came to his wife's room.

"Your god exists, mistress: the voice of the child and her reading were extraordinary."

In an angry voice she responded: "How did you hear it from Dürnev's room?"

"I did not go. I came to the inner door to hear, and I didn't leave until the end."

Selim Pasha smiled at an image that came to life in his memory. When a concubine opened the door, from the gap, he had seen the girl hafiz in from of the reading-desk, between two long tremulous candle flames. Her gold-colored eyes were open, inside them burned an undulating green light. He had become aware that the lines of her long child-face, which he though out of place and insipid in his wife's room, were sharp and regular. This pale pink face, how it appeared to fly out of an ancient Persian miniature!

"That voice must fall into the hands of an extremely good music teacher." "What does the Imam say?"

"He should be glad, the value of the girl increases if she becomes a hafiz."

Selim Pasha, twisting and turning his beard, thought of how beautifully that voice would read the semai[13] songs of Dede, and muttered to himself:

"A voice made to recite the old composers."

"Heavens, Pasha, the Imam will never let the girl sing a song? In his opinion, singing songs is a sin."

"The songs that I meant men like Dede, like the sultans composed … They are all pious… There are limits to the power of a neighborhood Imam to disapprove …"

While Selim Pasha was explaining to Miss Sabiha at great length how he would train Rabia's voice, the door opened and Hilmi entered.

On the faces of father and son, wherever they ran into one another, the self-same expression appeared. Hilmi's brow knitted together lightly, Pasha assumed a mask that was half contemptuous, half indifferent to hide his malediction, his inner bitterness.

The Minister of Justice saw his son as an example of a Pashazade, little effeminate Pasha's cut from one and the same block at the same time like minted gold quarters. His dress was not dissimilar to theirs. He gave an excessive importance to the creases in his pants, his waistcoat and jacket were cut impeccably. But in spite of this, the deepness of the colors he selected, the fact that in his neckties he was never a prisoner of fantasy, showed a difference, a

---

[13] An Ottoman lyric poetry form, 8 syllable lines, 3 to at most 5 quatrains, subject matter: nature, beauty separation. (Source: http://www.kultur.gov.tr/EN/belge/2-17335/variety-within-minstrel-literature.html)

tranquillity in his taste. His face at first sight was like that accursed example. Very tiny elegant mustaches, a face that was bloodless, thin, a little degenerate. But if you paid attention, there were two elements in his face that kept him from foppishness: the first being his eyes and the expression of his glance, the other, his mouth and the attitude of his lips. His eyes were different from other eyes because they were characterized by thoughtfulness, even the absentmindedness of men thinking deep thoughts. The lines of his mouth were clean and clear, the ensemble of his mouth dwelt cleanly on his lips, there was the sweetness of a man of refined disposition. From the Pashazades with their wide shapeless lips, made ugly by the sexual perversions of their lives and their dissipation, this mouth full of love and power at once distinguished him. But this Selim Pasha did not perceive. This son, who in no way resembled the somewhat predatory creature possessing his own blood and soul, in destroying the desires of his life would frustrate the example of his generation. Was it possible to see anything good in him?

Hilmi gave a cold but polite greeting to his father. One by one he took the two hands of his mother, kissed them. After placing them on his head, he held them thus for a little while and brought them near his cheek as if he was expressing not only respect but the depth of his love.

"Your girl hafiz is a real find, mother!"

Miss Sabiha trembled from love that the son had shared a thought, an opinion, with the father.

"Your father thinks so, my child."

Hilmi, lisping a little more from emotion, or as if recoiling from being of the same opinion as his father, said rather exaggeratedly:

"What a contralto . . . what a rich voice ... But how monotonous . . . How she reads resounding like an Egyptian Arab . . . He must absolutely save her from a constant legato!"

Selim Pasha neither knew the meaning of contralto nor of legato. But he liked the style of the girl. He did not want to emend her characteristics, but to publish them in a more prominent shape. He asked ironically:

"How is the voice saved from the thing you call legato?"

"If it were up to me, I would immediately hire Peregrini as her teacher. In two years, that voice will become a miracle ...Who knows, perhaps she will become a 'Prima Donna' on European stages. But it cannot be ... we are old fogeys ..."

His eyes moistened with longing for the image of an unattainable civilization where "Prima Donnas" sang songs on stages.

After Selim Pasha had said to himself "The boy's a fool," he began to be occupied with the thought of Peregrini. He was a European who taught piano in Europeanized families. Selim Pasha, at first obliged to keep him under surveillance for giving piano lessons to gentlemen in the Palace, soon after left him alone because he had come to the opinion that he was harmless, although perhaps a little crazy. In any event he was a fellow with a pointy beard and devil face who was very much unlike the other European piano teachers. He spoke Turkish like a Turk, he was reputed one of the most knowledgeable men in Istanbul concerning Eastern philosophy and culture. He was said to have abandoned his fatherland and his religion.

In fact this was hardly unfounded, because when he was a monk in I don't know which worldly monastery in Italy, he ran away from there and came to Turkey. The Pope's agent was continually making propaganda against the fellow, annoying Selim Pasha. His friends even related that he practiced religion in secret. But Selim Pasha, carrying the portfolio of Minister of Justice, considered suspect every relation that did not express a clear meaning. How different a man from the temperament of Selim Pasha . . . Pasha was of the opinion that the rascal was irreligious, and according to him every man who abandoned his religion was suspect.

"Does Peregrini train all the women who do the performance trade on European stages?"

"I did not want to say that... Naturally it is difficult to explain this point to you, how could I describe the refinement of European music, you could never be able to appreciate it, because..."

"Who said? There was no time when a foreign troop came, that I was not at Tepebash. The fact of the matter is that, as Minister of Justice, to see to what extent the people long for foreign goods... To listen to the end is a little difficult but there is a group of fops, a row of spectators whom it is really worth every trouble to watch. The rascals are beside themselves..."

"Everyone who knows about real music naturally . . ."

"Real music you said? If they did not have dispensations from the sultan to perform, I would grab both the harmonica players and the spectators and toss them on the pavement of Beyoglu. They are a bunch of half-naked, impudent old European women who sing like train whistles. Their eyes jump out of their sockets like those taken to the Palace and they scream like March cats. If she ventures to practice the Toptash saz, to sing traditional songs, this would be a more proper work for her to do."

"Why do you argue about a subject you don't understand?"

"Look at me, Hilmi, stop being a know-it-all, listen to me. You remember you said that both European music and European literature represented life. But let me ask you, in life have you seen a man making a declaration of love with such a tumult of words as he plays the orta oyunu?"

"Let me know, have you never seen a dying man? I have seen many. But I never witnessed anyone who made such a long and uproarious speech. A man who fights for his soul should shake his arm or leg, should cry out . . . Is this life? And why do you recommend that pointy beard, the rascal whose past is unknown, to teach one of these buffooneries to our Imam's grand-daughter, the little hafiz?"

Hilmi, as if he did not hear his father, said to himself:

"The Westerner making Western musicians … in them there is life, there is technique."

"What fault do ours have?"

"The people's laziness, their narcotic contentment, that the upper classes dive into low and unchaste debauchery, all these things are the effect of our groaning, weeping music. The stupidity and abasement of our women …"

"Do not bring in the subject of women. Ours in any event are more well-bred, more ladylike … In their males and also in their women I for my part have seen nothing else than shamelessness and insatiable eyes."

Pasha stopped, coughed and then spat out:

"Why do you take every opportunity to insult the tradition of a Moslem nation, its civilization?"

"It is not our civilization that I insult. Like Ziya Pasha said, the Western lands that you insult are prosperous places full of mansions; the property of Islam is ruins from end to end . . ."

"May their mansions collapse on their heads. Impious one, like a rascally traitor to the sultan you equate mansions and prosperous places with civilization, damn you!"

Pasha paused; he yawned. Why had he gotten into this debate with his lisping son? Was it of any value? His head was a weather-vane caught by any strong wind from Unbelieverland!

"Let me entrust the education of the little hafiz to the teacher whom I want. You are a child; when you become the master, do as you wish. I am afraid children are like the puppet girls of Asim Bey ... like a department store doll . . . When you press their tummy they sing out mama, papa."

This was the last attack. Without waiting for Hilmi's answer, without giving any importance to the anger and malice burning in his eyes, he left.

Miss Sabiha inhaled. She stroked her son's arm.

"Why do you go against your father, my son? A father who has not hurt you in any way, has not flicked you one flick, one thing is not the two that you have said..."

"I wish that my father was from the race that takes a beating every day ... I with that our house was not a mansion, but a hut... There is splendor, there is ostentation, but I am ashamed of my father, mother, you do not understand, I am ashamed. Bloody murder is the tool of the tyranny of a sultan... When I think about it, I am there in my mind."

Miss Sabiha thought to herself: "He was graduated first from Galatasaray. But what difference does it make, he is still a little clerk in Maliye. His monthly allowance does not even suffice for the tailor. If his father did not approve, where would he get the money to spend?" But she did not say anything to Hilmi. There was nothing that she would not have done so as not to hurt this only child whom she loved the best in the world.

Hilmi thought to himself: "All the suffering of my mother, collecting parasites, buying jewels, throwing money away in the street . . . This insane extravagance of women creates tyrants like my father." But he too hid this thought from his mother. Whatever happened, she was his mother and she was the only person he loved in all his world. Indeed this weakness that he nourished towards his mother was the reason his hands and feet remained bound, that he could not rouse himself to action. His shoulders sunken like those of an old man, his voice filled with despair, he was saying to himself:

"The wheels turning the state are unsound, community life is rotten, and our women . . ."

His mother interrupted:

"Why do you continually attack women?"

"Why should I not attack them? Each one is a tool useful only for pleasure or for bearing children . . . To which of these shall we say a human is a tool for? Even if the chains are golden, they are still captive . . ."

"Do you say so! In this famous Europe of yours men must bear children... But also there it is their wives or their mistresses who give birth. A little later, you will say that a rooster lays eggs."

In these stressful bitter minutes the cold mocking words of his mother... Hilmi continued, stuttering more and with a growing darkness inside his eyes: "Half of the nation, the other half, is occupied with satisfying its animal appetites. Let whoever bears children, bear them. I wish they would hatch like chickens from an egg. But look for once at how their minds are brought up. The rich, they are gilded creatures, boasting of their pure breeding, operators, empty headed, while the poor like a herd of animals are pitiable slaves... It isn't possible to see one among them full of thought, since..."

"Everyone goes through an ordeal when women talk, you are talking nonsense. What has a

44

woman done for you? Dürnev…"

"Dürnev, Dürnev… She is empty-headed and she is a sex machine. Our room has turned into a female fair. In the morning and evening it is full of outsiders shaking their hips and navels. Look at me, mother! If you send that Circassian girl as soon as possible to the Palace, what will you accomplish…"

"Why do you hate Kanarya so?"

"It is not even a matter of hate. I am irritated because… If you keep this girl in the mansion any longer, I will be with Dürnev and I will throw the girl into the arms of my father."

Miss Sabiha shivered as if she had taken a cold shower. Was the gossip about Dürnev and Kanarya true? Was Hilmi's irritation with Kanarya jealousy? Moreover, why was the boy such an enemy of women? Although her thought was a rather confused and tangled mess among "from what cause" and "for what purpose", she was fixed on only one point. That Kanarya would be presented right away this week to Her Majesty and leave the mansion was a critical necessity.

45

Chapter Seven

A fair crowd comes to the Friday Selamlik[14] to see the pompous and splendid procession, the elite and beautiful attendants in their rich and colorful uniforms, different types of horses shaking their manes and stamping the ground, magnificent carriages. As all of these things pass by in front of their eyes like a moving stream, each one individually is a nimble and quick to and fro within a scenic decor that leaves the opera in the shade.

But behind the curtain of this show, the spectators do not see the side that causes poor Selim Pasha to shake and sweat. His role in this pageant is big and complex: firstly, to keep people from shooting a bullet or throwing a bomb at Abdülhamid II, the head atop the body of his loyal slaves and lords; secondly, to see to it that the grandiose procession pass without incident; thirdly, to see to it that the procession pass securely and safely for the sultan, who was afraid like a nightmare of the official business of every selamlik; fourthly, to read the lies composed every week by the multitude of spies trying to earn their pay and by the journalists who want to earn money by exciting the suspicion of a tyrannical monarch.

On Friday's, as soon as the Sultan's carriage entered the Palace gate, Selim Pasha took a deep breath. Usually, he was admitted to the presence of the sultan and he always returned to the mansion with a big red satin moneybag in his pocket. Friday evening was when Pasha received callers. But at no time on that day did his visitors guess that there was a ford in the Pasha's life. This last Friday, after the other guests had gone, Pasha detained the Imam and raised the question of Rabia's education.

"I have found it worthwhile to appreciate the religious education you have given your granddaughter," he began.

---

[14] The procession of the sultan to the mosque.

"Your servant is one of the teachers whose speciality is to educate the hafiz, Lord Pasha."

"Thanks be to God, your granddaughter is both intelligent and gifted. One thing has come to my mind. A procession of teachers come to the mansion, Arab music, Persian music, French music, etc. And there is no one who has benefitted very much. What would you said to having Miss Rabia benefit from them?"

The Imam rubbed his hands, coughed but did not answer. Pasha continued:

"If perchance you should think it fitting, other than the evening hours when she has come to Mistress, the child should come to the mansion at one in the afternoon."

"Your servant has given education and study coming from my hand. God forbid, that I should object to the wishes of Lord Pasha, but . . ."

"But?"

"The child says her prayers five times a day. And it is known, the young people of today are all irreligious, if Rabia should be separated from the eyes of her mother …"

"The people of our mansion perform their prayers five times a day."

"Of course, of course … I did not mean to say that. There is a further question … I have made the child dress in accordance with the sacred sharia. And it is known, one peer is led astray by the other. In our time, their women, what is called 'mode' which is contrary to religion …"

Pasha interrupted the Imam a little roughly:

"We are not going to change the child's manner of dressing."

"I would like to present another matter which is of trivial moment for the Lord Pasha, but is vital for poor people. The child reads the response in Ramadan, in ordinary days is invited to chant the Mevlit[15]. Your humble slave ekes out his household economy with the child's earnings. If perchance ..."

"I will speak to the bailiff. He will ensure that you do not see any loss from the education of the child."

The Imam was contented. Not only for the money, but also since because of Rabia he would have a place beside influential men. And in spite of all Emine's objections, that week the Imam began to send Rabia to the mansion on a regular schedule. In this new life, it was as if Rabia had been transformed and freed from slavery. She no longer took lessons from the Imam, she no longer had to listen to his chatter about Hell and especially his unseemly words concerning her father. No longer did the Imam own the child as his own property; he became someone who took pride in her. Although in the mornings she still saw to the housework, and was forced to listen to her mother's grumbling, after lunch she left the house and only came back to go to bed. Now the Imam would intervene in Emine's nitpicking, and would scold her: "Daughter, prosperity has come to our house, keep it short and don't nag the child."

Even though she did not begin her lessons in the first week since she began to pass half the day in the mansion, she began an education in life and the etiquette of life that is not learned from teachers. Especially to be by Miss Sabiha's side was to be thrown into the fountainhead of life; it was as if while life was continually changing its shape she took life by the hand and looked it in the eye.

In general, she would convey the orders that Mistress gave to the mansion people; thanks to this she got to know the mansion people well. Very often the child's delightful face, her friendly eyes, would soften those pieces of information that were harsh and she would not tell the sometimes belligerent and insolent answers of the mansion people to Mistress. This

---

[15] Prayer for the dead.

reticence and calm won over even Dürnev, who had at first adopted a contemptuous and aggressive tone. Especially on the day when the list of honors came out, Mistress would send her to Pasha's room several times, would have her investigate in return for what service a so and so bey or pasha had been honored. Rabia would find Pasha in his room, wearing his accustomed damask cardigan and white nightcap, carving a back-scratcher with the calm of a man who possesses a clear conscience and a happy heart. In the middle of groaning as if it came from the bottom of a well and muttering old songs in a deep voice, he would suddenly stop and joke with the child. He was very funny when he explained the real story of the reason for the honors. His nose stretched out with sarcasm, its tip hooked like the beak of an eagle, he himself laughed inwardly. When Rabia heard these reasons, her mind was turned topsy-turvy. Every type of favor was a treachery, mischief was similar to a prize. One day Pasha said winking one eye: "Tell your music teacher, that he should teach you "O golden pleasure"!

"I have not yet begun to practice, Lord Pasha. What does it mean, golden pleasure?"

"Golden diversion!"

"Is this not the song that Miss Kanarya sang?"

"You young scamp like you . . ."

Why, I wonder, did Pasha find this question of the child strange? Pasha's laughter stopped and his face grew serious:

"Next week they will put Kanarya into her gilded cage . . . She will no longer sing songs in our mansion . . . "

"Really?"

In Pasha's chatter, she felt a sense of foreboding for the beautiful girl whom she well loved and with whom she ate all her meals, and her face clouded up.

"Why are your eyes full? It is not bad. She will go to the Palace, she will belong to the Palace. The golden cage is not such a bad thing, my daughter."

In Rabia's mind the Palace at once became a gilded cage. A place where beautiful blond girls sang the song "O golden diversion" while leaning against the bars of the cage.

The next day when Miss Sabiha had sent her to Pasha's room she found Kanarya there for the first time. Pasha was sitting in a straight-backed chair, his face appeared worried, his eyes abstracted. Kanarya on a floor cushion playing the oud was singing in a full and sad voice a song which Rabia never forgot.

"To whom should I make a complaint of the heart about you?"

"Heart" was prolonged like a thread from the girl's mouth, the strings of the oud under the girl's white fingers took up the melody with the same sadness.

When Pasha saw the child, he was a little annoyed: "Does Mistress want something?"
When Rabia explained, Selim Pasha's face appeared as if he wasn't taking it in: "Tell Mistress, this evening I myself will explain the matter to her."

When Rabia had left the room, the two called after her with one voice, summoned her back. Kanarya made a place for her on a corner of the cushion. The young Circassian, her head bent with a secret sorrow and a heavy grief, her voice hoarse, was weeping tears drop by drop from her eyes to her cheeks. At the same time, she succeeded in smiling with her lips.

"Next week we will not eat together, Rabia, but when I get established in a Palace, I will invite you," she said.

50

A short while after, Rabia rose, and this time, when she had left the room, Pasha also came with her to the antechamber and said slowly:

"Don't tell Mistress that Kanarya cried . . . Don't say anything about seeing Kanarya here, it is better that way."

....

Three days after this adventure, Rabia passed in the mansion a happy evening that dazzled her eyes. All the chandeliers were lit, everyone had put on long skirts and silk kirtles, there was no lack of swishing silk in the antechambers. That evening, Miss Sabiha was giving a banquet for Her Royal Majesty, Kanarya's future mistress, and after the banquet she would take Kanarya, the living gift that was presented to her, and carry her off to the Palace.

In the salon behind the curtain a Turkish band was playing, everyone was waiting for Kanarya's singing and dancing.

They had made a high platform in the room for Her Majesty, on top of it they had placed a gilded armchair.

The woman, a crown on her head and on her neck a brilliant neckband with a single stone, was sitting alone in the chair. On divans opposite her, with their medals and jewels, huge feathered fans in their hands, the ministers' wives had been arranged partly according to their husbands' office and partly according to their relations with each other. But it was the palace women who occupied Rabia's mind the most. The old maid-servants were below the platform, the young ones were in the middle of the doorway, strolling about in the antechambers very coquettishly.   Each one had taken their long skirts on their left arms, on their heads a topknot pulled down dangerously close to their ears as if it would immediately collapse . . .   Each one was speaking a mangled Circassian that more resembled the language of birds than Turkish. Each one had one up-turned eyebrow, they all looked like stone dolls turned out quickly by one and the same artist.

When the band struck up a dance air, Kanarya was taken into the room. She had on a rose-colored shalwar[16], a tight purple velvet vest and slippers the same color as the shalwar. The shalwar had been embroidered with gold and silver sequins. The long sleeves of her tulle shirt and its broad cuffs waved like two wings; her golden hair pouring down her back under the chandelier was like a silk shawl. Immediately she began to snap small yellow bells on her fingers, then she jumped, she turned, like a musical wind and as if her legs, her arms, her neck were the band she trembled, bent over, straightened up. In the midst of all this movement her body kept a strange perpendicularity.

The dance, the band, the voice all came to an end and the palace people left. Her Majesty walked at the front; at the back was Kanarya. White veils over colorful overalls, in the middle of the veils, in a frame of kohl, watching blue, green, hazel eyes… Their flashing appeared to Rabia as if it came from some creature other than man. Kanarya's blue eyes sent their last greeting to her.

Everybody descended to the courtyard to see off the guests. Through the gap in the doorway one could see the outer gate of the garden. Rabia saw the black-jacketed harem lords, the grooms with their colorful ornamented uniforms who opened the carriage doors. The black coupés swallowed up the palace caravan. This was the last passage of this blond female procession before Rabia's eyes.

Miss Sabiha asked:

"How did you find Kanarya's dancing?"

"Very beautiful!"

---

[16] Baggy oriental trousers.

Miss Sabiha raised her eyebrows.

"Who says? Like a peacock very stupidly she turned, she strutted. If you saw the dancing of a gypsy named Penbe . . .

Chapter Eight

Rabia began music lessons with Vehbi Dede after many Arabic and Persian lessons. Miss Shükriye said to her: "Kiss your teacher's hand." When she had left, saying, "This is your new student, Sir." to Vehbi Dede, the girl remained in the middle of the room where she had been pushed. Rabia's cheeks burned like fire, she said to herself: "Where are his hands, I wonder?" but lacked the courage to go forward.

Where would she find Dede's hands to be kissed? Certainly they were somewhere in his harmin, which (although she didn't know this yet) was the long camel hair cape stretching from his neck to the floor that dervishes traditionally wore. Why didn't he also extend his hand like the other grown-ups? She raised her eyes very slowly to her new teacher. Dede's long neck stuck out a little from inside his harmin, and his head inclined to the left underneath his kulah, the conical dervish hat; his attitude was that of a man waiting for something.

When the child's eyes at last found Dede's eyes, two scrawny hands emerged from the harmin; he crossed them over his chest and gave Rabia a dervish salute as if she were a grown-up.

Rabia smiled at Dede's elegant attitude, at the unusual expression on his face, as if she was seeing something new. Vehbi Dede's eyes were intense and looked outside with a child-like confidence, his face resembled a triangle, with its broad forehead and pointy chin. His nose was slender and regular, his lips a little mocking, with a patchy reddish- brown beard that although sparse on his cheeks became abundant towards his chin.

Dede pointed to a floor cushion and said: "Sit, my girl." Then he bent down, and, placing the child's hands on his knees, he opened her fingers. With this action Rabia's tension left her body and she relaxed, a little peace came to her emotions, the violent beating of her heart and her fear passed away. After throwing his harmin on a cushion, he dragged another cushion opposite the child and sat down. His shalwar was threadbare, the elbows of his shirt were patched, the pile was worn away from his sleeveless vest. But in spite of this poverty of appearance, his manner of dressing overall gave a different impression. Right then in that minute the lesson began.

"Dim, tek tek, dim, tek tek . . . " As he was saying this he made the child's hands strike his knees. When the child had grown accustomed to this simplest of rhythms, he took a ney[17] from the divan and began to blow a simple tune.

Thus passed Rabia's first music lesson. As the days passed and Vehbi Dede taught her this music that was very different from reading the Koran, she grew accustomed to its strong internal pulse and made it her own. And after teaching her to strike the most complex rhythms on her knee, her teacher put a tambourine in her hand. The harmony of her voice supported by her fingers as they wandered on the taut skin and gave the beat went well with the tinkling of the finger cymbels.

When Emine heard her practicing the tambourine, which she insulted calling it a "gypsy instrument", she assailed Rabia angrily to her father:

"Let's look more carefully at this mansion and see what those impudent rascals are teaching the girl . . . for money you will make your granddaughter a gypsy musician."

The Imam stroked his beard.

"Who has you play the tambourine, Rabia?"

"Vehbi Dede."

---

[17] An end blown flute, one of the oldest musical instruments, with a sepulchral haunting tone color.

55

"Fie, woman, Why do you stick your nose in a business you do not understand? Vehbi Dede is a saintly man. The dervishes do not play the tambourine as an instrument for worldly pleasure[18]," he began, and then entered into a long explanation.

The fact that the Imam took Rabia's side in the matter of the tambourine meant that she was left unconstrained in her music lessons. And after the tambourine, the child learned the oud, the zither, almost all the Turkish instruments, with an aptitude and speed that left Vehbi Dede astonished. And after a time she played the stringed instruments, although not as skillfully as her teacher, with a fire, an exultation very much peculiar to herself.

Henceforth, on the evenings when she remained in Miss Sabiha's room supposedly to read the Koran, she would always sing a song. Exhausted from a long day of practicing, she went to the old woman's room, leaned her back against the divan, stretched out her feet, her tambourine in her hand, and her sweet voice would jump from song to song. Most evenings Selim Pasha would also come, send for his nargile, listen to her, and the harshness, the toughness of his face would depart and, his eyes intent on something far away, he would smile to himself.

Of all the inhabitants of the mansion, it was Hilmi who pursued with the most interest by far the progress of Rabia's continuing music lessons with Vehbi Dede. From time to time he felt pain great enough to cause him to tear out his hair, at the sacrifice of that beautiful voice to tired old folk songs. But whether he wanted to or no, when the girl sang a song, he too was drawn to his mother's room and he exercised his imagination thinking what a peerless form that beautiful voice would take at the hand of a teacher who was a master of Western music like Peregrini.

Every Thursday evening -- because Pasha passed those evenings until midnight in his apartment --Peregrini came to the mansion, congregated in Hilmi's room, chatted and gave a

---

[18] In the whirling dervishes, the tambourine – being circular – is a symbol of the universe.

concert. Hilmi, barely eight months after Rabia had begun to take lessons, decided to have Peregrini hear the girl, and after obtaining his mother's permission, Miss Shükriye brought Rabia to Hilmi's room.

When Rabia's feet had brought her upstairs, they were going quite slowly. She was a little afraid of Peregrini. She had followed with deep attention the argument about vocal education between Selim Pasha and his son, she did not wish in the least to pass from the hand of Vehbi Dede whom she loved very much to Peregrini. She entered the room treading on tippy toes.

In front of the piano four people had gathered. Hilmi was sitting in a chair, standing on one side was a tall, sharp-featured dark young man, on the other was another young man with a faded blond complexion, behind Hilmi leaning his hands on Hilmi's shoulders was a hugely tall man. These, in spite of being next to the piano, were chatting about everything but music. In particular the dark man -- one of the public works engineers, Shevki Bey -- gesturing with his hands repeated continuously the names of Mazzini, and Namik Kemal.

The footfalls of the child vanishing in the soft pile of the rug were perceived first by the delicate ears of Peregrini, who suddenly turned around. He was a small and thin man whose dry face had been covered suddenly by spreading lines like a spider's web, his eyes were hollow, his eyebrows thick, his beard pointy, his black neck-tie with an artist's negligence covered half of his chest, perhaps thirty or forty years old.

"This child of ours will become an artist," he said and stretched out his hand to Rabia.

The girl -- perhaps being accustomed to kiss every outstretched hand, perhaps not knowing it was his custom to "squeeze" hands, or perhaps thinking him a Moslem because of his faultless Turkish -- kissed the hand of the artist and placed it on her head. The young men snorted as they covered their mouths with their hands. But Perigrini appeared pleased. In his mind the child awakened immediately a comparison with the rich, Europeanized girls to whom he gave lessons. All of them were like straw paper copies of European children; whereas this girl, with her three tight pig-tails down her back, her open face and buff-colored scarf, was an indigenous example created by the centuries-long evolution of the culture and civilization of the city of Istanbul.

Her eyes, honey colored with green spots, were serious and dignified. There was serenity and power in her mouth with its somewhat big pink lips. The eyes of the piano teacher shrank, a smile coming into life on his lips deepened all the lines of his face. Rabia smiled involuntarily. The others argued over what song the child should sing for the master. Hilmi with a finger on the piano began the song "To whom shall my heart make a complaint of thee?"

"Let me have her sing this one," he said, "she sings it beautifully."

The master shook his head.

"Is not Mademoiselle a hafiz who reads the Koran in mosques? Let her read read in her own style from her own book."

Three young men found this thought of the master "très original" and immediately they set about creating a mise-en-scène. The blond youth -- Galip, son of Osman Bey, who was a member of the state council -- brought a reading desk which he had found. Shevki lit two candles on top of it. Hilmi brought a white lace head covering that he snatched from his wife's room. He covered Rabia's head. Peregrini, carried away by the scent of theater in the air appearing between the tremulous white candle flames and the girl hafiz's narrow face in its white frame, turned down the lamp that was on top of the piano. Suddenly Rabia's face, in the middle of objects diving into shadows and opposing one line to another in the dimness, seemed like a picture of the Virgin Mary. Then the master said rubbing his hands together:

"Beatrice would have looked just like that the first time that Dante saw her."

58

The eyes of the three young men were fixed on Peregrini's face, so as not to let escape the impression that the child's voice made on the master, but his were fixed and stayed on the girl hafiz.

Perhaps for one long minute the girl's body waited motionless as if turned to ice. Then inside secretly like a water of life beginning to flow her head and shoulder at first imperceptibly began to undulate, then her whole thin body, and a strange and profound harmony began to flow in half and quarter sounds from her lips. When she began with the "bismillahi", this movement and sound was low and light, but as it went on it grew more powerful, the beating of her heart grew stronger like a fevered blood vessel and at the very last moment in the concluding formula "sadakallahulazim" it slowed down and suddenly was cut off.

Now the little hafiz, as if frozen, having let slip away the power that clutched her body when she was reading, was lifeless, spent.

Three pairs of eyes were a little amazed at the impression that this scene, which was so habitual for themselves, produced on Peregrini. They thought him a philosopher, irreligious like every philosopher --certainly they thought his irreligion as powerful as the Muslim fanatics who are blind followers. Now he, hanging his head, humbling his inner expression, looked like a priest doing penance for his sins.

When he raised his head, there was no trace of haste or exaggeration in his manner. In an enthusiastic voice he said to the child:

"Can you tell me the meaning of what you read?"

Rabia shrugged her shoulders. She had not yet gone far enough in her Arabic lessons to explain this.

Hilmi again ran out. From Pasha's library, he brought back a book of commentary whose leaves had turned yellow.

While he said the Turkish translation of the verses that Rabia had read, the pianist, having taken his notebook from his pocket, was writing them down:

"The Lord, to the angels: 'We will send someone (Adam) to be judge of the world', when he had spoken, they replied: 'When we are full of raising your holiness on high and of praising you, shalt thou send someone who will create mischief and spill blood here?' "

The pianist put his notebook back in his pocket. He said:

"See here, it was this stumbling-block, this objection of the angels that was the very thing that separated me from God, from cloisters and monasteries."

Hilmi and his friends were silent. They were seeing him from a new and altogether different perspective. It was his sedulous pursuit of currents of thought in the West rather than his pursuit of knowledge found in Eastern sciences that had made a powerful impression on the minds of his young students. But they loved him the most for his irreligion, because he had abandoned his church and his order. They imagined themselves free from religion because they saw the religious as an obstacle to every change, to every jump forward. Because of this, they believed there was a friendship of thought, a oneness of belief, between them and the ex-priest Peregrini. The sympathy that the artist showed for Rabia's Koran reading confused them a little.

Hilmi asked: "Do you not want to educate this voice, cher maître?"

Rabia's eyes burned with rebellion, but Peregrini calmed the girl in saying with sincerity: "No, it is necessary to render unto Cesar what is Cesar's, and unto God what is God's... I am from the class of Cesar, of Satan. The child is God's, let her remain in her place."

One week later, Rabia went up to Hilmi's room on the orders of Mistress. Peregrini and Vehbi Dede were chatting face to face, as usual. Dede was calm and unagitated, the pianist was full of fire and movement. Peregrini was talking about Satan, from whose class one week earlier he had claimed he was. Satan and God, these were topics that Rabia had heard about in her surroundings every day since she was five years old. She did not find it strange, she sat down and listened.

Peregrini was saying that: "Did not Satan cause Man to eat for the first time of the food of the tree of knowledge? If this had not happened, the sum total of man would have remained a creature who eats, drinks, walks on two feet. Curiosity is the key of all learning, and it is Satan who was the first owner of this key and who first gave this key to us."

The pianist waved his hands while he was talking, raised his voice, his eyes each one like a search light were wandering over Dede's face. But Vehi Dede heard him out, watching the enthusiasm of a child with an adult's calmness, or perhaps indulgence. The pianist continued: "If this had not happened, affirm the courage of Satan, Master Dede. Thought is the patron saint of courage. He was the first who rebelled against the creator, the first of everyone who eyed a jump from the blessings and easy circumstances of heaven. And think of Prometheus stealing and bringing his first fire to the face of the earth, he is the patron saint of all philosophers, of all great revolutionaries, even of ordinary men like me who rebel against their church. See what a beautiful piece I have composed for Satan."

He raised his hand in the air, and lowering them to the piano, after first saying: "A toast to the honor of him who sacrificed being a famous angel in heaven for the sake of freedom of thought!" His frenzied fingers began to wander over the piano.

It seemed to Rabia that in the air which he struck all the satans and demons of the universe, untied, drunk with freedom, were screaming and clamoring.

The blond Galip clapped his hands.

"If we teach the people in this country to worship Satin for the sake of becoming accustomed to think, how would it be, master?"

Shevki grumbled. He would always thrust Galip's words into his mouth.

"Beware, lest I imitate the master, in my opinion don't start talking about Satan to the people; they will think you went to an orta oyunu with Zuhur[19]."

"Monsieur, don't you make a mockery of whatever I say. Moreover I was speaking to Vehbi Dede. He is like no other pilgrim of the hadj or Islamic master. What do you say, Mr. Dede? For the sake of progress shall I exalt the name of Satan?"

Dede smiled very sweetly.

"In my opinion, there are not two powers called Satan and God in the universe. Each one, everything, is an appearance of one single truth, of one single power. From molecules and atoms to the most enormous suns, from man to insects invisible to the eye, each is the work of one single creative power. Good-evil, beautiful-ugly, God-Satan, these are invented names. Behind each there is one power who itself has created itself and is continually in the work of creation . . . He, he . . . is a creator who continually creates to reflect his shadows on a curtain that is called 'universe' . . . His name is Allah, Rab, other names. There is one thing only that is a retort to his secrets, a place that is the most brilliant place of his light, the one that least has a beginning, Love!"

After saying these things as if he was reading a Mesnev[20] he recited a line from an Persian makam: "Enough love, permanent desire!"

Peregrini was still crying out with the same excitement: "Grudges, hatred, fighting, scrapping,

[19] Zuhur seems to be a general term for any actor in the orta oyunu. Zuhur is an Arabic word for stage appearance. Zuhuri was also the name of the most famous Istanbul orta oyunu company.
[20] A philosophical verse by Rumi, the 13th century dervish poet.

brutality … Is it not necessary to put up with these since any evil is the work of God?"

"No …each one is the same shadow of light, each one is the same different paints that the divine painter has used …"

"In that case, Dede, you don't believe in a different and individual soul."

Dede shrugged his shoulders. "Is a droplet that becomes a fountainhead, or a fragment of light that becomes the sun, are they or are they not individuals? I have come to believe only that there is a huge oneness that takes us inside itself as a piece of itself. No one on this side of the curtain can perceive the other side."

"In that case?"

"In that case, it is sufficient, the further side of this. All existence, all lands, even the heavens that exist in the solar system each one is a shadow, a temporary shadow play."

Peregrini's eyes softened, Shevki's beetled brows joined together and Vehbi Dede read a Turkish translation of a Persian quatrain in a sing-song voice: "Sit drinking in the pubs; drink, burn my altars and set the Kaaba on fire; but oh human don't harm me in any way!"

Finally Vehbi Dede turned to the ex-priest and in a low voice finished his thesis:

"I have very much wanted to learn the 'from what' and 'to what' of existence, Signor. But never have I seen it under one single form, in the condition of a 'slave'. This huge play never rests for a moment, is always changing, changing . . . Come Rabia, my daughter. On his road the traveler is a necessity. And before leaving let us sing our song."

Rabia took up the tambourine, Dede the ney. The girl hafiz – according to the concerns of the world and the ambition of the world -- changed her cardigan and abaya[21] and sang a song of Galip Dede, the greatest of the Dede's. She began to sing:

"Again my heart has fallen on its side and broken.

Then the last lines, which summarized all of Dede's philosophy, finished with a sadness that confused everyone's heart:

"One man abandons fame and renown; another has fallen into it."

When Vehbi Dede and Rabia had left the room, Peregrini asked: "This miracle child, whose daughter is she?"

Hilmi explained: "Her father is a vagabond who plays the woman's role in the orta oyunu. This country has never seen an artist caricature woman in so realistic a manner."

"Did he die?"

"No, but the girl does not know her father. At the time of her birth, her father was exiled. No one but my mother still remembers this clown."

Peregrini remembered Yorick in Hamlet. Kissed in life, Yorick's mouth was full of earth in death.

"Why was he exiled? Was there a connection with politics?"

"In what way? The man was not one who would know about such things. He fell victim to fanatics and conservatives. Apparently his roles contaminated our social traditions. Finally he committed an act against propriety ... unseemly ... As usual, by the hand of my father he

---

[21]A collarless woolen overcoat.

was exiled to Galipoli."

The quality of bitterness produced in Hilmi's voice when he spoke about his father if anything this time was more profound. He was quiet for a while, then continued: "The child resides with her grandfather. Cursing his ex-son-in-law five times a day in his prayers, he is a neighborhood Imam who does not know how to talk about anything besides Satan, hell, hell-hounds. And don't try to see him, master. He is a religious of a quite different stripe than Vehbi Dede. He calls you, even us, infidel and if you invited him he wouldn't come."

"In any event, invite Vehbi Dede again for the coming week, Master Hilmi, he is a very appealing man. The air that he played is the most beautiful song melody that I have as yet taken down."

"The element is dangerous," Shevki muttered.

"Why, Master Shevki?"

"In my opinion the Imam is less detrimental to our country than Dede. The narcotic, soporific toxin in the philosophy of the dervish is much more dangerous than the fairy- tales of heaven and hell of the Imam. The Imam only repeats a type of fable that superstitious beliefs gave birth to; Dede removes the difference between good and evil. He promotes the concept of an artist god who uses something called paint on tableaux of good and evil. Do you know what is the logical consequence of this belief? Its believers become tolerant and indifferent to tyranny and cruelty. For instance if the public comes to believe: 'The actions of our Red Sultan are all done as God wills ...' How many men will we find behind us to overturn this despotic regime? If you ask me, the dervish lodges should be removed from this land first of all."

"You speak like a future nation-builder, Master Shevki. Dede has no relationship with the nation. His domain is the soul of the individual . . . a soul that has curiosities, enigmas, hunger, thirst particular to itself! Whether or not men are composed of small pieces of an apparent nation like some type of world-womb, they return naked to the congregation. Dede has no relation with the future Turkish regime that you have imagined."

This evening for the first time Peregrini looked at his young friends from an altogether different and very serious aspect. He had always considered them a little "bookish", a little "snob", rich heirs without work or power who chatted of rebellion only to pass the time. This evening the openness in Shevki's thought especially made him think. I wonder whether some secret historical powers are on the verge of opening a new track for the Turkish nation by means of these talkative, imitative youths? Hilmi was the model of an impotent Hamlet with that head all jumbled up, thinking unnatural things. He was a Hamlet insofar as the image of a thousand and one ghosts did not impel him to violence for a fixed ideal, or even to the littlest movement. But how different from him did Shevki appear! The pianist was murmurring to himself very weightily.

"Perhaps for new epochs one needs destructive and fiery men . . . to construct a new building the debris of the old must be swept away . . . But I wonder what would have happened if men like Dede had not been one man in the crowd?"

"Why are men like Dede absolutely necessary, master?"

"In this world of trouble and tyranny, the spirit of the individual sometimes needs peace, beauty, consolation. Moreover only secret powers can provide that."

"In the machine of a state that is well set up, an individual has no need at all of consolation. The mischievous philosophy of mystics like Vehbi Dede creates weak, dreaming, and particularly inimical souls. We will set up the state for ourselves so that neither trouble nor tyranny will exist there . . . We will crush the head of every power that would spoil the health, the equilibrium of our state."

Galip rose to his feet, and said: "Abdülhamid thinks otherwise, Monsieur."

Vehbi Dede and Rabia left the mansion together. Their eyes were on the torch that Shevket Aya shook lightly in front of them. They walked together until the corner where they were to separate. They grew silent and tasted the summer night overflowing with calm and beauty. When they parted, Dede pointed out the heavens to the child:

"God this evening has lit all his lamps."

Rabia even after Dede had gone remained in the place where she was and her eyes stared at the heavens. In her heart there was the emotion of someone waiting for big and happy events. What silvery summer evening in Istanbul doesn't give the sensation of being on the eve of great events to the heart of man? God's innumerable candles, spread out on and clinging to the dark blue dome, to what friendless vagabond have they not shown the way with their friendly points of light?

At the corner of Sinekli Bakkal Street, there was a sweet scent. In the deepest shadows of the purple wisteria arbour hanging over the fountain like a purple wave, in the sound of droplets falling into the basin was a harmony that deepened the silence.

They should have turned right at that moment into the street where the gate of the Imam's house was. But both Shevket Aya and the child preferred to pass from one end of Sinekli Bakkal Street to the other.

In the distance only a few dogs were barking. But the street was completely asleep. Shevket Aya suddenly stopped in the middle of the street. "I wonder why there is a light in that window this evening?"

Rabia raised her head to the window the servant had pointed towards. All of a sudden her heart began to beat violently. The lighted window was over the grocery shop that had been closed for years . . . The window of her father's house. She grabbed Shevket Aya's hand, pulled on it:

"I wondow who is there?"

"Perhaps a thief has broken in."

"Come on! Let me go see."

"Impossible."

The child's agitation touched Aya's heart a little. This man, who had been in Pasha's service for fifteen years, knew the inner workings of Sinekli Bakkal by heart. The two heard the cudgel of a watchman beating the hour in the distance, and they raised their ears, waited. The watchman Ramazan Aya approached striking again and again the pavement:

"Merhaba, Shevket Aya."

"Merhaba, Ramazan Aya. Have you seen the light in that window?"

"Isn't that Tevfik's house? He has been back for a week. He'll probably open the shop for Ramadan."

The watchman passed on. But the eyes of the child remained glued to the window.

Her heart was jumping with a booming noise from joy that overflowed from its root, her hands pressed down over her chest on her heart.

"Come on, let's go now, Miss Rabia."

Shevket Aya simply took her by the hand, pulled her. "Certainly, Mistress has spoken to Master Pasha, he will have him sent for …"

Rabia did not listen. Tomorrow, she was thinking, tomorrow she would see her father.

Everything suddenly had changed, the world had become the most beautiful of dreams. A yellow pregnant dog that always waited for her in front of her gate sniffed at her skirts, thrust its soft neck into her knee. Rabia hugged the dog's neck, and said with a dry sob:

"Sarman, Sarman, my father Tevfik has come."

After pulling the gate's cord, she dove inside. In the courtyard she stopped and waited for a while by the small gas lamp. She was praying that her mother still slept after she pulled the cord.

Chapter Nine

In the morning Rabia turned into Sinekli Bakkal Street swinging her produce bag back and forth. In a flash she arrived at the midpoint of the street, she stared at the shop. The sign "Istanbul grocery" had been repainted and someone who had stopped at the shop gate was raising his head and looking at the sign. He was a strange creature. He was like a child, but not dressed like a child. On his back was a long pink robe, on his head a cotton turban … Hearing footfalls behind himself, he suddenly turned and Rabia came nose to nose with a middle aged dwarf. In his wrinkled face, he had the depressed eyes habitual among comics.

"Tevfik, a customer has come," he called to the interior of the shop.

A tall man bent his head low to be able to pass through the gate and in that old street came face to face with the small lovable customer he had not expected. Green spots in golden eyes were glittering with fire, the face framed by the white head covering was flushed with an emotion that Tevfik could not explain.

As soon as this man came out of the shop, Rabia warmed to him. Her eyes fixed on his hot chesnut colored eyes, together with the laughing mouth under the long brown mustaches, she too was laughing.

"The shop is not yet ready, but never mind. Please come in! little mistress. Let me make a siftah[22]. God willing your arrival is auspicious!"

Rabia held up her basket, showing him that it was overflowing with beans and onions. "This morning my shopping is finished."

"Well, well, tomorrow morning you will buy from us."

---

[22] The first sale of the day, considered a sign of good luck.

"Every morning, every morning ..."

The emotion in the voice of the child left Tevfik a little puzzled. A cyclone blew into his mind. Whom did this girl resemble? Emine ... Although her lips were narrow, her eyes were not small, but the narrowness of her face, the evenness of her complexion . . .She had been this girl at the same age. The voice of the watchman Ramazan Aya was still ringing in his ears:

"Your daughter has grown a lot, Tevfik! She has become a hafiz."

"What is the name of your father, my girl?"

"I am Tevfik's daughter.

A few things happened at once. The dwarf leaned on the gate and was crying. Tevfik had overflowed like the River Danube, like a typhoon he was turning around his daughter, snatching her and raising her up in his arms, he was wandering upstairs and downstairs in the shop like a crazy man, from time to time he would let her go, then after looking in her face he would cover her again, in turn he would cry and rave as if he was crazy.

When he had found a little bit of calm, he made Rabia and the dwarf sit on a soap box, himself between them, one of his arms around the waist of one, the other arm on the shoulders of the other one, he hugged the two of them together, he was loudly kissing them in turn. In this happy accident, Rabia was still the most in control of herself.

Tevfik's child-like spirit, the crooked and pitiable body of the dwarf were two miserable friendless wretches desiring their needs and expecting love . . . Rabia laid claim to both of them together.

As soon as Tevfik sat down, he began to describe the years of his absence and the homesickness he had felt in exile. A disordered and confused story, but vigorous and living enough that Rabia felt she herself had passed those years with her father. In the poverty of the first years in order to earn a little money he entertained the people in market places; sometimes all alone, deprived of a roof to lay his head, he wandered hungry and a vagabond, his eyes and mouth watering in front of bakery shops . . .

When Tevfik saw that the happy eyes of the girl cried at this part of the story, he jumped to another phase of his exile.

"When Zati Bey became governor of the sub-province of Galipoli, the face of the exiles laughed. I at once found a job by his side, my head was given a place, my back clothes, my belly found hot food. But oh! I earned all of it by the sweat of my brow. Both inside and outside the house I worked night and day."

"May god grant him good health! But was he not afraid of the sultan?"

"What do I know, my sugar! The other exiles did their own trades, they said. Supposing that he gave a good conduct to the exiles, he was afraid on the assumption that he was a supposed Young Turk, and he gave him a civil service post. Supposedly he had been a high official in Istanbul, and became a type of exile-governor . . . supposedly, supposedly, supposedly . . . If you understood, there would be wheels within wheels."

Tevfik winked an eye to explain more clearly these confused speeches, but Rabia still did not understand anything. Lest he cut off his chatter at this point, she shook her head as if she understood.

By day I took water from the pump, I led children bringing them to the school, I even picked vegetables. But when the evening came, come on! dried fruit in the gardens ... Until morning, striking, exploding, hitting, playing . . ."

"And then?"

Tevfik paused, he tried to think how to explain the unseemly and obscene divensions of these nights. He said to himself:

"There was a gypsy dancing woman, pock marked, a used-up face, but what a devil, what a devil."

Rabia, remembering Emine, said in a dry voice: "To say Gypsy is to say Bad Woman," she said. Tevfik's face clouded over:

"Don't say that, Rabia, a thing supporting a man's heart in her chest, that Gypsy came there. If it had not happened, what would I have become? A dog, a bear with a hoop attached to his nose and made to play to entertain the lords . . . A thing, she put me in a man's place."

"If it was thus, then she is not a bad woman. But you, when did you come, Tevfik? For a long time now, everyone had talked to her about her father calling him Tevfik; thus it became natural to her to call her father by his name. But she had such a lovable way of saying "Tevfik" that every time her father would hug the girl and kiss her hair.

"How did they permit you to return to Istanbul?"

"Haven't you heard that Zati Bey has become Minister of the Interior?"

"Ah, Ah . . . "

"He brought me. And he also gave me a little money."

"What have you been doing until now?"

"Looking for work. The Zuhuri[23] orta oyunu company has split up. . . Most of their friends
became 'actors'. Ha ... ha .... ha! How is this 'playing'? They learn from books
they have read.   My sort of intelligence has not attained to this. If the player cannot adapt
and discover what he shall say right at the moment, if he doesn't know how to do this, will he
not play like someone who reads suras of the Koran from memory?"

Tevfik was angry at the splitting up of his old friends, and especially at their playing works in
translation inside wooden theater shacks. There is a type of intelligence that does not reach to
awakening interest among our people in strange lives and foreign worlds. In any event, he was
very pleased that he had found his oldest friend Rakim, a famous dwarf in the orta oyunu.
From now on until death he would not separate from him. At once he placed the dwarf on
his knee, and starting on a new topic he introduced him to Rabia:

"See, here is your six fingered uncle." The eyes of the dwarf came to Rabia as if he was
begging forgiveness for his crookedness, his disability, his ugliness, as if a little love was
begged for. How they were like Sarman's yellow eyes! She wrapped her arms around the
dwarf's neck, kissed him on both cheeks. But at once the dwarf turned this into a mockery.
He rubbed the places she had kissed, cackling drily. Rabia rushed off because there was
nothing left to say, she set about inspecting the shop. She thrust her nose into every sack,
every box, and sniffed.

"From now on we shall open the shop. Perhaps I and Uncle Rakim, we two will make an orta
oyunu company and gather up money. These Ramadan evenings we shall play Karagöz. If a
man does not make a little chatter, his tongue rusts."

Rabia was listening as though she had lived her life in Tevfik's shop, was giving advice
about the arrangement of shelves. If Rakim had not overturned her vegetable basket and if
the onions had not rolled about on the floor, Rabia would never have woken from this sweet
dream. Alas, it was almost noon. If Emine nagged her even when she returned on time from

---

[23] Zuhuri was the most famous orta oyunu company. See note 18 on page 79.

the market, what would she say today? She snatched up her basket, rushed from the shop, running as she turned her head back she said:

"I'll come again after eating."

Tevfik stood in the shop's gate, he waved his hand, a good while after Rabia had turned the corner he was still waving his hand.

Rabia came back and began to clean up. She inserted the back flaps of her kirtle into a sash, and putting one bare foot on top of the wooden back of the brush, the other on the floor; one hand on her waist the other in the air to keep her balance, she began to scrub the room over the shop. Rakim also was barefoot, and in his hand was a rusty leaking bucket overflowing with water from the well in the garden, which he poured on the floor wherever Rabia pointed to, like a shuttle-cock between the house and the garden.

In the shop Tevfik was busy putting the finishing touches to his Karagöz production, once in a while he would call out … The three were as happy as children.

Busying herself with many years accumulated dust, grime and dirt, Rabia's heart was as light as water. For the first time in her life the walls of prohibition had been pulled down to their bottom. As if a hand, untying her heart-strings, had said: "Laugh, play, love and live as much as you want!"

That morning when she returned to the house at noon, she received a very powerful scolding from Emine. After her first meeting with her father, which she found so sweet and loving that it penetrated her soul, suddenly her mother seemed loveless and her heart full of rancor.
Whatever Emine asked her, if she wanted her to explain why she had been out so late, she responded with an equally stubborn silence. Perhaps Emine would have beaten her, if the Imam had not stopped her in time. But this stubbornness, provoking Emine's garrulity, so that she said that if her daughter had a fault it came from her father, although it opened her

mouth about Tevfik, shut her eyes. For the first time Rabia looked into her mother's eyes with rebellion: "Both I and my father are evil . . . What can you do? Please, let me go to my father," she screamed.

"Your father? Look here, if he puts a foot in Istanbul, I will lie down under the sultan's carriage in the selamlik, scratch at the doors of his council and explain how worthless that wretch is. If I do not have him exiled again to a corner of Hell, let them not call me Emine!

Rabia was terrified by this and her lips were sealed. She made a decision to go straight to the mansion so as not to hint to Emine that her father had returned. But again she was not able to resist, she turned back from the mansion gate and came to the shop.

Now she was pondering as she scrubbed the boards almost powerfully enough to tear them to pieces. It was not possible to hide from Emine the fact that her father had come. So? The child reminded herself that Miss Sabiha was the only place of security against this danger. She would explain to her, she would take shelter in her. At once that evening she would tell her. Whether or not they had noticed that she had not come to the mansion after noon, she would go to eat in the evening, and after eating she would pour out her heart to Miss Sabiha

That evening becuase Miss Sabiha had guests Rabia did not say anything. The next evening she did not have the courage. The fact that Emine very seldom went out into the street, perhaps on rare occasions visited neighbors' houses, kept her unawares of Tevfik's return. The mansion did not pay attention to the fact that Rabia did not come in the afternoon. This situation lasted for a week.

On every day of this famous week, in the afternoon Rabia came, cleaned the house over the shop, going into the kitchen she put it in order. Her father, the dwarf, and she became very accustomed to one another, they became unceremonious as if they had lived together for years. However, when they thought about what would happen if Emine learned of this situation, their merriment vanished. But Uncle Rakim explained to Rabia that there was a process of judicial election between her mother and her father, Rabia swore that she preferred her father, and Tevfik's face was laughing.

Every day before this adventure of Rabia was discovered, the three passed the most happy hours. Finally the house was ready, the shop was white-washed, scrubbed clean, the goods arranged each in its place, the shelves were decked out, covered in colored paper up to the ceiling, hooks were hung.

And Tevfik's Karagöz production was ready too. The three fixed a place in the garden for the curtain, and a place for the lantern. Ramadan happened to be in Summer. Its evenings, dangling God's lamps in the thick dark blue dome, were going to laugh at the sins of the world, a thousand and one minarets would make the mahya[24] lights sway in the warm and sweet air of Istanbul.

Tevfik said: "We do not have a tambourine to make the necessary commotion."

Rabia jumped in: "Let me bring one from the mansion. I know both how to sing songs and how to play the tambourine. And moreover, you will be entranced by how I beautifully I play."

Her youthful father narrowed his eyes, laughed at his daughter's swagger. But suddenly he shook his head in vexation.

"You are a hafiz, Rabia. How shall you sing these types of mummery? Where has a hafiz been seen who sang: "When the beloved diverts me, the beloved.""?

"Only hear me play once, and then tell me . . . I am a student of Vehbi Dede."

"His work is wasted here. Your art is not suited for street children, for someone who plays a

---

[24] Lights strung between minarets that spell out Islamic inscriptions or symbols.

neighborhood Karagöz."

Rabia grinned and plunged into the kitchen. A minute afterwards her long fingers were strolling over, playing a tambourine made from a tin coffee tray. Her father snatched the tray from her hand, shouting at the top of his lungs:

"I did not tell you how I loved nine lovers," he sang and at the same time with the most clamorous rhythm he was playing the tray. Then he threw down the tray; to his daughter he said:

"How would it be if I also bought a monkey for you, and you played in the streets?

Since there is this aptitude in you, piles of piasters will rain on your head from windows, and we will make pocket money."

This joke of her father reminded her of the days when she watched a monkey from a window. When her eyes watched the gypsy as flexible as putty, she ached so much to join the procession of children in the street that she would press her nose flat as a pancake to the glass.

She bent down, took the tray from the floor. Suddenly she became a gypsy making a monkey play. She wandered about the garden, striking the tray very precisely and very harshly, her head to one side, her chest thrust forward, one of her feet kicking a monkey, making it play. Rakim did not trust the artistic performance of the child. He also at once became a monkey. Walking on all fours, turning his eyes to all sides, crying like a monkey, jumping as if he was snatching nuts, throwing the husks in Tevfik's face as he cracked them, from one side of the gypsy to the other he jumped from side to side turning somersaults.

....

That week ended with a comic theatrical scene of the following sort.

It was not until Thursday that the bailiff's wife learned from Vehbi Dede that Rabia had not attended her music lessons that week. Every evening she would see the child at table and after eating in Mistress's room. A so industrious and well-mannered girl would not neglect her lessons … In that case surely Emine must be detaining her in the house. Immediately she covered her head and went to the Imam's house.

It was afternoon. When Miss Shükriye knocked at the door, Emine was bleaching laundry and her ear was already on the alert . . . Rabia's mind and manner had been quite different lately.

When she opened the door with her hands full of soap and the bailiff's wife was suddenly there, the first person to greet her after the morning, asking her why she had kept Rabia from her afternoon lessons, she was puzzled. "Rabia is not at the mansion?"

"Nooooo . . . She has not come in the afternoon for one week."

Emine's eyes narrowed, two stinging needle points, she pursed her lips until they became one narrow line, and she told Mistress Bailiff what was coming into her mind.

The girl, last Friday, after coming home late from market, fundamentally a worm had entered her heart. She had passed through who knows what disaster. Fie . . . what a pity it was. Saying 'we will educate the virtuous virginal daughter of a poor family' they took her to the mansion and abandoned her to the streets? Is that your 'mistress'?

She was in a total lather when Miss Shükriye said that Rabia was just a child. Her breasts were like apples on her bosom, she was a big girl who was approaching the time when she would see her period. Mistress had abandoned her only child to the streets and taught her smoothing gel, rouge, kohl, lesbianism and other things. She shouted at Mistress Bailiff that she was a lying blabbermouth, a cuckolded woman.

If the Imam had not started from his afternoon sleep because of this racket and run downstairs, the two women would have fought in the courtyard hair to hair and head to head.

Miss Shükriye went back to the mansion without learning where Rabia had gone in the afternoons. But from the moment she set foot in Mistress's room, a row began. Rabia was there, finally telling Miss Sabiha about her father's return. While she was speaking, Emine came to the mansion. If during all these events Miss Sabiha had not shown her sang-froid and her ability to take charge, some dreadful disaster would have happened. When Emine, coming, her mouth frothing, to level a full frontal assault on Miss Sabiha, heard about Tevfik's return, she suddenly fell down in a faint. As soon as she had come to, she jumped on Rabia's throat to strangle her rather than give her to that clown. While the whole mansion tried to restrain Emine, Miss Sabiha sent word to the Imam. After a discussion with the Imam at the Mabeyn door[25] , the decision which they took was the following:

Sharia, at any rate to a child of this age, had given the option of deciding whether to go to her mother or her father. Rather than sending the matter to the law court, was it not more suitable to settle it amicably and make Selim Pasha the judge?

The Imam at once gave his consent. The protection of Tevfik by the Minister of the Interior Zati Bey, the fact that it had come to the attention of Selim Pasha his political rival, if it were possible to turn it to his own advantage, to lightly fan the flames of this rivalry and to obtain a post for himself by this strategem … This seemed to the Imam a most suitable outcome. And Mistress's keeping Rabia in the mansion until the outcome of the trial seemed the most suitable side of the matter.

After the Friday selamlik, after a long discussion with his wife, Pasha passed into the men's quarters and received the Imam. Today Mr. Hadj Ilhami appeared like an old man, with aged

---

[25] The door separating the harem, or women's quarter, from the public, or male, quarter, the selamlik.

eyes and a twisted neck. He said: "The decision that our Pasha will give, I am prepared to accept as the judgment of Sharia. I am afraid that the child will want her father. Truly the thing that I am upset about, is that after so much trouble and work the worthless rascal will take an innocent child of his to the house of a drunkard and ne'er-do-well like Zati Bey."

Pasha's dense eyebrows suddenly drew together. "I will tell Tevfik not to take Rabia to Zati Bey's mansion. If he should take her, the girl will no longer set foot in our mansion."

The Imam rubbed his hands, lowered his voice: "Also let me show the court that the neighbors were astonished as to where Tevfik got the money to open the shop . . . Everyone says that he is registered as a spy for Zati Bey. And in Sinekli Bakkal he is certainly not spying on poor people like us."

Pasha laughed. He understood at once the Imam's stratagem. "Leave politics to great men, Mr. Imam. As for yourself mind your own business . . ."

This time the Imam did not insist on politics which were in his opinion delicate. He laid bare his true purpose and anxiety with a frankness that saddened Pasha "If the child goes to her father, her earning from singing in the mosque will be gone as well. We have expended so much money, so much trouble. And if the income that the child brought in shall have been cut off, we will be half-way between hungry and full. It is well known, there is no fear of God any more in the world. With a poor Imam like me, the neighbors bargain over every certificate like Jews."

The Lord Bailiff, meanwhile, took Rabia, and then Tevfik, into the room. Pasha at first said to the child:

"My girl, you see here your father and your grandfather. By the side of which do you wish to dwell?"

"There is no one else for me but my father."

"Do you have the power to provide for your daughter, Tevfik?"

Rabia jumped in: "We will open the shop, Lord Pasha. Everyone will buy from us. And you will buy from us, won't you?"

Tears flowed drop by drop from the girl's eyes. The Imam was losing the game. He gulped:

"He has fixed his eye on the girl's earnings, he has unfairly influenced her mind, has he asked after or looked for his child once in so many years?"

For the first time, Tevfik opened his mouth:

"May you keep giving Rabia's earning to the Imam, my Lord. I will provide for my daughter."

This proposal appeared suitable. Pasha sent Rabia to the harem, dismissed the Imam, but kept Tevfik back.

"I am much occupied with the education of your daughter, Tevfik . . . Will you permit it to continue?"

"If it is your command, Pasha."

"In that case, I make one condition. You shall not take you daughter to Zati Bey's mansion."

"God forbid!"

That was to say that the moral lapses of Zati Bey were unbecoming even for a tramp like

82

Tevfik.

Pasha coughed. "Tell the truth, Tevfik. Did Zati Bey give you a job in the neighborhood?"

"How do you mean, a 'job', my lord?"

The astonishment on Tevfik's face was genuine.

83

Chapter Ten

The shop life of the three was like a day that precedes a feast day. In their opinion, Sinekli Bakkal, with its broken pavement, its foul smells, its darkness, had become with joy alone the center, the soul of a living universe erupting in a great booming noise. They played with life like kittens with a ball of silken thread, never yielding to the thought that one day the silken threads could get caught on their hands and feet.

The "Istanbul Grocery" again became the busiest place in the neighborhood for bargaining, the number of customers surpassed by far the number in Emine's day.

Rabia was the leader of the three, but Rakim was their intelligence and organizer. When a week still remained before Ramadan, a constant and informal visitor caused additional merriment and gaiety in the shop. This was the Gypsy Penbe on her return from Gallipoli. Under the pretext of diverting Miss Sabiha, she had overstayed her welcome at the mansion, and once a day she would be sent to Sinekli Bakkal, where she would joke with the women at the street-corner and after quarrelling with the children would plunge into the shop.

Rakim had gone to buy merchandise, Rabia to the mansion. It was Wednesday afternoon. While Tevfik sat alone in the shop, a tall Dervish sheikh bent his head and entered the store.

"Is this the shop of Mr. Tevfik the father of Miss Rabia?"

"I, Tevfik, am at your service . . ."

"I am Miss Rabia's music teacher. I want to speak with you."

"You must be Vehbi Dede."

The dervish laughed. "This is the thing I wanted to say: I don't give lessons during Ramadan. I don't often go to the mansion. I would like to make an exception for Miss Rabia, because in thirty years I have not come across such a talented student. If there is a suitable place here, I will come and give her lesson on Thursday evenings."

This meant that Rabia's music lessons would be transferred from the mansion to Tevfik's house, that Dede would give free lessons to Rabia . . . Tevfik's chest swelled from pride, his eyes became moist:

"What a favor for us! Won't you relax and drink a cup of coffee in our garden?"

"Let me come another day, I must be keeping you from your work."

"No, Master, at this time there is no commerce."

Tevfik opened the back door of the shop. He ushered Dede through a tidy and clean kitchen into the garden. He had him sit on a rush mat under a walnut tree; after leaving a tobacco pouch in front of him, he went to make the coffee.

The garden was the only place that Tevfik made an effort to tend lovingly. On one side of the walnut, growing very close together were fig, almond, apple and quince trees. On the other side, at the bottom of the wall, were fields of eggplant, tomato, onion, and lettuce … Dede turned his eye to the house. The window wrapped up in leaves suspended over the kitchen and arbour was painted in blood by the setting sun. Beside the arbor, hugging the kitchen door, woodbine and jasmine wafted a narcotic odor in the heavy air of evening. There was no other sound but doves cooing on the branches of the acacia trees to the left side. A perfect Istanbul garden. Dede was able to imagine himself in his own garden.

While they slowly sipped the coffee that Tevfik brought, he was studying the house's owner, and was finding him very similar to himself. This continually speaking child-faced man was one of the vagabond children of God. Dede had seen all sorts of different kinds of them. Although most of them had led stormy lives full of adventure, they were old acquaintances who had entered into the throng of believers and, on the threshhold of the dervish lodge, they had left behind the pleasures as well as the insults of the world. Dede, when he left the shop, looked on Tevfik as a future soul-mate of the path.

Two weeks after, when Rakim was alone in the shop at noon, another stranger came, quite different from Vehbi Dede. The dwarf opened his eyes because he had not become acquainted with such a man in Sinekli Bakkal, and he gave the stranger the once over. Dressed in a long cape, with a huge three cornered hat, he was a foreigner of short stature and a nimble attitude.

Because the Christians of Sinekli Bakkal did not wear hats, Rakim conjectured that this was someone quite different, a customer from Begoglu or perhaps a traveler:

"What would you like, Signor?"

Peregrini, who did not know what bashfulness was, entered somewhat bashfully. Although this ex priest was an apostate from the Catholic world, he had passed fifteen years among Moslems; however, all his Turkish and Moslem friends lived in a Europeanized and wealthy world. To this man, who was regularly admitted even to the Palace, until now the home of a poor or middle class Moslem was closed like a fortress. But this artist, coming from an altogether different social class, began to be powerfully interested in this small new shop that he had entered with trepidation. Here the heir of a city of ancient civilization felt pleasure in the eye that disposed colorful merchandise with a special care for Ramadan. While he was strolling with the dwarf amid green and red beribboned wafer wheels hung to the ceiling, his eyes jumping like a rubber ball, Rakim asked, and asked again:

"What would you like, Signor?"

He pointed to the wafers with his finger:

"I want to buy one of these, one with the red ribbon, one with the green . . . "

He had not gone there with the intention of buying anything. But this was not a bad way to find the time to talk.

Rakim, as he was wrapping the wafers, suddenly put his eyebrows together. There was no relationship between the fellow's dress and the wafer. Moreover, there was no relationship between his dress and his ability to speak Turkish. In that case?

Maybe the fellow was a spy? They said that sometimes they went around in disguise. His suspicion evident in his voice, he asked very sharply: "Do you know how to cook it?"

"No. Our cook is Greek. Perhaps he also does not know, but I still want to buy these white rounds. You, will you describe how it is cooked?"

Peregrini took a notebook from his pocket. As he was writing, he began to explain: "I am Selim Pasha's son's piano teacher."

"Oh …"

Rakim took heart.

"Vehbi Dede is my friend. I heard Miss Rabia in Master Hilmi's room. They have not come for two Thursdays. They said that Miss Rabia's father had come. He is said to be an artist, and you look like an artist, are you her father?"

"I do not know what an 'artist' is, but I am not her father. I am her uncle." He stopped. In spite of the strangeness of his dress, he had warmed to this fellow who spoke Turkish so beautifully. His voice was a little bitter and a little mocking when he added:

"Meanwhile, I have become Rabia's monkey. The girl is very clever. Although Vehbi Dede does not give lessons during Ramadan, for her alone he comes here Thursday evenings."

Peregrini took a small chair, sat down.

"Miss Rabia is said to read the response in mosques. I wonder which?"

"Today in Hagia Sophia, Saturdays in Fatih, Wednesdays in Valide Mosque, other days in the Sinekli Bakkal masjid. She earns heaps and heaps of money. But all the money goes to the Imam. Thus Pasha has decreed. We have our grocery business here, we will put on Karagöz this Ramadan. Thanks be to God, we will subsist."

He paused a little, his eyes shining with a question:

"Signor, you will not find a puppeteer like Tevfik in any corner of the world. If you want to come in the evenings, I will let you in for free."

"Let me come at once, tomorrow evening, my friend."

He had said this with enthusiasm. Now in the place where he sat, having fixed his eyes on the street, seeing what appeared to be a black cloud in front of the gate, he perceived it was black flies continuously buzzing. The houses opposite were as if asleep under their black eves; this hour of fasting the neighbors would assuredly pass in their beds, because no mortal would pass through the street.

The joy of those who have found a secret and closed continent had enveloped Peregrini's heart. A lovable, personal, informal and human continent! He had perceived this world for the very first time when he heard Rabia read the Koran. At that moment everything external to this shop and street was artificial, unnatural. Thus it came to him that for the residents of this narrow street there was not a single physical value in the world, but they valued only the heart, spiritual riches and beauties.

As soon as he had come to this opinion, his desire was awakened to hear Rabia inside the historical decor of Hagia Sophia. With a strange smile spreading from his lips to every line of his face, he said:

"Will you take me next week when Miss Rabia reads the Koran in Hagia Sophia?"

The corner of Rakim's eyes grazed the three-cornered hat, which was in his mind the most particular indicator of blasphemy.

"When the congregation worships, it is not customary to have foreign visitors."

Peregrini, following the direction of Rakim's eyes, took his hat off his head and threw it on the ground.

"I will go hatless. I have a fez at home. And also I will not come to this neighborhood any more with a hat on. I will be very respectful of religious feelings . . . I, I myself some time ago was a sort of dervish."

"Or did you not become an unbeliever after being a Moslem some time ago? It is not for no reason that you speak our language so well."

Peregrini had forgotten that Rakim was merely a simple uneducated fairground actor. He had found it natural to entered into philosophical arguments with him that he simply didn't understand.

"No, I am not a Moslem. You remember, are there not priests closed up in monasteries? I was one of those. But now I am rather more a Moslem. Fifteen years I have lived among you. Language, religion, nation these are nothing else but spiritual climates of people The Western spiritual climate became very cold to me. I am looking for peace and healing in the climate of the East ..."

Peregrini stopped talking. Rakim said to himself: "What jumble of things is the rascal mixing all together?" But when he began to speak again, Rakim opened his eyes, and listened.

"I do not belong to any one religion. But if I wanted to acquire a religion, I would certainly become a Moslem. I find that the individual in the congregation that Islam has created is closest to myself. It is fifteen years since I ran away from the monastery, since the Pope excommunicated me . . ."

"You ran away? O mother . . ."

"Now I do not believe in anything. However, religion like a sickness once it has entered the soul of a man does not leave. I love religious people very much, I am enraptured by religious talk. I promenade outside of churches, mosques, all places of prayer. Are you religious, my friend?"

"Thank God I am a Moslem. But I in no way like religious talk. I balk at churches, in the mosque my soul is bored. If I hear a sermon, I go to sleep. I am afraid of pious men as if they were bogey men. I have never said my prayers. Rabia's father is the same way . . ."

"You don't say your prayers in Ramadan?"

"No, and we two only fast superficially to save the girl's feelings."

"How, for example?"

Rakim laughed. He took pleasure in pouring out his inside to this old unbeliever who had escaped from a monastery.

"In the evening together with Rabia we eat the sahur[26], we make niyet[27]. The following day until she goes to the mosque we eat nothing. We do not look for food, but is there not this unbelieving tobacco? As soon as she has gone to the mosque, we bring out the tobacco boxes, we smoke cigarettes. From this and that we gobble food. In the evening with Rabia again we break the fast, we eat iftar[28]."

"Strange, strange . . ."

"Sometimes the girl suspects. Among us, fasting men are addicted, disagreeable; we however are all merry. But in the evening I will really fast, for the sake of Rabia's feelings."

"Why not for the health of your own soul?"

The dwarf grinned. A bitter, tense grin. "Do children fast? Monkeys especially do not fast. God created me a creature somewhere between a monkey and a child. Neither prayer, nor vow, nor fast from me…"

After this visit, on the Thursday evening when Vehbi Dede came, Peregrini also came. As was very natural, Hilmi and his two inseparable friends accompanied the master. In the poor room above the shop, there began to be debates resembling sixteenth century scholastic arguments.

．．．．．

---

[26] The meal just before dawn in Ramadan.
[27] The solemn vow to fast.
[28] The evening meal during Ramadan.

91

It was necessary to make a very deep and very close examination of Rabia's face to see what effect her new life had had on her spirit. But it was not an examination worth this trouble, because her old and her new life were like two strata of civilization camping out one on top of the other and completely corrupting each other.

The expression on her face of a child not moving and pressing together her will to live like an internal gun-powder cellar had not been completely erased. When she fulfilled her responsibilities in her capacity of leader of the three and lady of the house, despite taking pleasure from these things, and despite considering them a little bit as play, her manner was still tranquil and serious.

Rabia's old face: two deep lines by the two sides of her mouth, a deep line between her eyebrows, a worried heaviness enveloping her slender face. The new life, without erasing completely these lines, without changing the expression of her face, began to trace its footsteps over this old personality. And this was her new face: puckers produced in the corners of her eyes from frequent laughter, happy lights ever burning within her eyes, a lovable crease on her nose visible when she laughed. The traces of her old face which she had abandoned for the freedom of her new life became faint; the heavy expression of her eyes, the lines between her eyebrows and on the edges of her lips improved. But whenever her mind reverted to passed days, every old track came into view in total open shamelessness, as if the happy mask of her new life had been draped like a transparent silk veil over the sad expression of her old life. Thus the harmony of these contradictory things on that young face constituted its difference, which created the impression of a total enigma, a total magic spell.

Peregrini, who let no meaning that her face took from day to day escape his eye, was the first to make a very thorough analysis of Rabia. He would watch the struggle of contradictory expressions on that tiny face with the passion of a Spaniard watching a bull-fight. There was a tendency towards asceticism in the girl's character, an aptitude for spiritual fasting, an ability to think fast and take sound decisions. These all were works resulting from the harsh struggle and strict education of her first years, and of the inherited expressions that came down from the Imam and Emine. Many powerful things had passed to her from her mother whom she detested so. There was a dryness in the side of her heart that could not excuse in any way those who had given her pain, she was rancorous.

Rabia's sunny joyous sides, her aptitude for art, came from Tevfik. For more than eleven years, by day and by night, they had been trying to teach her the two concepts that were above all others, namely religion and the other world. But she, more connected to people and living things than to thoughts, was to become a woman who loved until death when she loved and whose heart was captured by the littlest act of kindness.

Peregrini, searching out every element of the mystery of this conflicted soul with the curiosity of a scientist testing elements in his laboratory, spoke with her whenever he had the opportunity, asked her questions, looked into Rabia's eyes as if he wanted to look into her brain and pierce the face of the girl with the small eyes. But that which most fascinated him was the girl's aptitude for music. Her ears completely preserved every note, her matchless voice gave back every note accurately and her taste was so honest and sound that it would content whatsoever master she had. For this reason, Peregrini would play every new composition of his first for her; he would ask seriously for her opinion, and listen.

Vehbi Dede was preoccupied with Rabia. But he did not show his interest like Peregrini. He did not struggle to analyze the girl like Peregrini, he accepted that Rabia's inclinations were a necessity of nature. As a result of his experience, Dede knew that every person is an alloy compounded of a thousand and one contradictory things. She had an honest judgment and tendencies to spiritual fasting that would restrain her ambition, and modify the God-is-to-be-praised exuberance of this girl whose heart was fiery and warm. Dede had begun to consider her as his spiritual heir, the future disciple who will diffuse and simplify his philosophy and thought for the people. Because of this, when he thought of Rabia he would say to himself: "The eagerness and love of her heart must not die, however her capacity for asceticism in her life must be protected."

Chapter Eleven

Uncle Rakim catches Rabia in the kitchen, asks her: "Whom do you love the most in the world?"

"Tevfik."

"Why?"

Can you know why? Who can describe heart strings taking root in the personality? Tevfik was the first sight of an oasis in a life that the child had thought was a dry desert, the only person to collect unfulfilled longing in his person. She seemed to find in him the tenderness of a mother that she had lacked, the strangeness of the imaginary friend with whom she wanted to play. Perhaps for that reason she saw to the needs of her father with such care, she sensed his wishes, at the exact time when she had poured out the ritual bath water of the Imam, she would prepare Tevfik's raki tray, and bring it to him at the same hour every day. But after bringing before him that forbidden and prohibited drink, she also found it natural to run and perform the evening namaz, saying "Do not omit thy mercy".

"Rabia, whom do you love after your father?"

"Vehbi Dede."

"Why?"

Can you know why? If she had known, she would say that Vehbi Dede was a holy pauper, understanding human weakness, forgiving, but over and above these things that he was a saint; she would explain that he gave consolation and power to Rabia because of this.

"Whom after that?"

This time after a little hesitation Rabia said: "Signor Peregrini."

Uncle Rakim's voice became finicky: "Why?"

Rabia also did not know this. If she had known, she would have said that her relationship with Peregrini was like a game of hide-and-side, it gave her fear and excitement.

"You do not love me as much as the infidel?"

The dwarf's eyes were full of despair like those of a wretched animal getting a beating from his master. Then Rabia's slender arms were wrapped around his neck, and she said:

"I love you by far the most of all, my little uncling, my monkey uncling."

.....

In the last week of Ramadan, Rabia saw Peregrini in the middle of the congregation listening to her response and wearing a small fez on his head. It was in Süleimaniye Mosque. It made her mind preoccupied with what Peregrini and what Rakim were looking at, as if worshipping something. Like every artist she was drunk with the excitement that art had aroused among the people.

The colored light filtered through colored glass struck against the oil-lamps of the dome overhead, opposite which the human mass pulsating as if with one single heart under this light was like a dream. But as soon as she noticed Vehbi Dede listening to her behind Peregrini, her tongue got tangled, her lips trembled.

This great master being a judge of religious music turned her topsy-turvy. She paused a moment, wiped the sweat of her brow with the tip of her head-scarf, began again. She thought through first in Turkish the verses that she read in Arabic, she would read them first in a voice that understood and explained.

"Like clay that the potter uses, He created man from clay and He created those heavens from a smokeless fire . . . God of the two East's, Master of the two West's... boats rising like mountains over the seas, everything upon the Universe is transitory, but the great and awesome face of the Master endures forever!"

Her voice embroidered a mosaic of a strange harmony from half sounds, gave a secret beauty to the verses and Vehbi Dede was thinking that the passage she read today, creating the foundation of Islam's mysteries, was more than just a product of chance.

After the response was over, Peregrini and Vehbe Dede went out; they looked at the pigeons in the courtyard for a while. The pianist was emotional, but he tried to turn the thing to mockery:

"If you put this child under the dome of whatever mosque and light two candles above her, she creates a music that confuses even an unbeliever like me. Whether God enters me, or Satan, I do not know. What art, what art!"

Vehbi Dede laughed. As if solving this question, very slowly he said:

"It is only at that time that the two contrary powers become harmonious in your spirit, they are tuned to an eternity without beginning in the artful mind of a child."

In the evening in the shop after Rabia had cut tickets for the procession of children and the elderly neighbors who increased little by little, she would go beside her father. The nimbleness, the skill of Tevfik's hands, giving life to pieces of paper, that his voice could become now a man, now a woman, now a child, in fact a woman, man, child of every type and social class, bewitched her. But the thing that most astonished her was the admiration of all the spectators for the almost savage harmony in Tevfik's voice, though he knew nothing of music.

Rabia would play the tambourine behind the curtain, and together with the dwarf, whenever genies, fairies and nameless spirits would come before the curtain, she would create mutterings, grumbling, groanings, in short all the noises that appeared necessary. In one of the chairs in front of the curtain, his fez appearing small for his head, Peregrini would always sit, and behind him, in the middle of the mass of children on the rush mat, Vehbi Dede's long conical hat appeared. But what most resounded through the garden was Rabia's merry laughter.

On the last evening, Tevfik distributed free sugar to the little spectators. And they massed in front of the shop striking over and over their toy drums and saying good-bye to Ramadan and to Tevfik by reciting in unison the couplet: "Lo it has come, lo it has gone." At last, shaking their lanterns up and down and illuminating here and there the broken paving stones, the collapsed eaves, they passed by and were gone.

Vehbi Dede said from behind them: "Everything is a moment, a moment in the light, afterwards there is eternal darkness . . . lo it has come, lo it has gone . . . the lifetime of a man, the life of the universe, seems to be a moment in the light, a fading image . . . a shadow play!"

After the guests had gone upstairs, the Gypsy Penbe and Shevket Aya came with trays of dried fruit in their hands. While they were preparing their fruit snack in the kitchen, a more chatty air than most evenings was blowing upstairs. Some were smoking cigarettes, others were still laughing, Tevfik was wiping his forehead with an enormous handkerchief.

Dede said: "Peregrini my friend, when Tevfik brought to life pieces of paper, how much did you think that he dominated the material of his mind? When thought goes, a man too becomes soul-less like paper, without meaning. This evening I was reminded of these words of Jesus: 'God is not a God of the dead, but of the living.'!"

Peregrini for the first time in his life did not want to enter into a philosophical discussion. He was trying to imitate Tevfik's voice when he came out and made the genies and fairies play. Galip was saying that:

"Listen to me, children. If we renew this thousand year old Karagöz with clothes befitting the times . . . For instance, if we bring the Red Sultan and his gang before the curtain, if we display their crimes, their outrages, would you say that there would be a revolution in the land?"

The dwarf's eyes flew out of their sockets:

"Lord Galip, don't malign the Sultan, or he will flay us all alive, stuff our skins with straw, and hang them out to dry."

Tevfik scratched his chin:

"You are worried for nothing, Rakim. In this period it is not possible to imitate the great; if a man imitates his own wife, they will exile him. I want to live and to die in Istanbul."

But his voice, hoarse from shouting, had become almost totally inaudible, his eyes filled up. He had suddenly remembered the prison he went to, the privations he endured. Through the gap in the door-way, he saw Rabia pass in from the anteroom with the plate in her hand.

"The kindness of great men is necessary for an uneducated friendless man like me, a blessing for great men at the beginning of each work ..."

But the power of art made him think in a secret corner of his mind of the stage which Zati Bey provided for him in his nights of Gallipoli debauchery.

Two months later, the owner of Cafe Kabasakal entered the shop. He had freshly painted the café, and covered it from head to toe in red velvet. Would Tevfik come once a week and tell stories? Lightning flashed in the eyes of the old player, he swallowed. The owner of the café at once surmised that he had accepted. But suddenly the fire in his eyes was extinguished, he shook his head and in an unyielding voice, he said: "It's impossible."

A week later the same man came again. He proposed that Tevfik would play Karagöz on Friday evenings. This time the black claw of fortune caught him by the throat:

"It will be," he said.

99

Chapter Twelve

When Rabia went to her father, the whole neighborhood opened its eyes. It scrutinized how the Imam and Emine would take the situation. But even those who could hardly stand Mr. Hadji Ilhami and his daughter, had to admit that they bore the situation calmly, and whatever their feelings may have been, they didn't color the day by displaying them.

The Imam nursed a feeling of expectation. Since the money that Rabia earned from being a hafiz came to his hand through Pasha's bailiff, he would have supposed that he had signed himself to a sort of truce with Tevfik and Rabia. He knew that no law would have granted him the earnings of his granddaughter. It did not suit his interest to spoil the agreement that they had made with the consent of Pasha and the two parties. His warnings to Emine were quite definite. She would never pass through Sinekli Bakkal Street, she would never discuss Rabia with the neighbors, she would not be rude to Selim Pasha's wife -- if by chance she should meet her in the street or anywhere.

Emine accepted these conditions whether she wanted to or not, and in the first months she satisfied the grudge that she bore toward Rabia by cursing her only five times a day.

But the interest and curiosity that she felt for Rabia and her surroundings, as the days went on, was burning up her heart. In any event, her hatred for Rabia was more intense than the rancor she felt towards Tevfik. If she without knowing it herself was awaiting Tevfik's return one day, that hope of hers now had been completely extinguished.

As far as Tevfik was concerned, though she hated him she had still considered him her property and was of the opinion that he would kneel down and clasp her feet the minute that she made the sign. Perhaps with time this opinion of hers was not very unfounded, but now it was certain that no time at all at been left to Emine since Rabia had gotten complete possession of her father.

In the middle of all this sadness, the prosperity of the Istanbul grocery, the happiness overflowing from there, sowed salt in her open wounds. A destitute and vagabond Tevfik, a remorseful and unhappy Rabia . . . Even if she had not forgiven them, she would have been able to remain indifferent. But their happiness becoming a neighborhood legend turned Emine's rancor, her veins, into fire. And the fact that she couldn't discuss this with anyone, that she couldn't pour out her heart, poisoned her utterly.

Four or five months after Rabia had left her care, in spite of the promise she had given the Imam, she began little by little to want to open her heart to the neighbors. But at that point the interest of the neighborhood in that matter had been relegated to the past ...
The neighbors would yawn and most using work as a pretext would slip off.

Even the Imam was sick and tired of the legend of Tevfik-Rabia. As soon as Emine opened this subject he would go to his room.

After praying, the woman would often lift up her hands -- as if she were face to face with a God who had descended from the heavens to listen to her -- crying, shouting she would lament Rabia's ingratitude and shamelessness, Tevfik's insolence, her own wronged state. But the Imam brought an end to this, her one and only consolation, saying:

"I say, woman, make your prayer silently; if the neighbors come, they will petition to have you shut up in the nut house."

On one of the days when she was thus half crazy, one of the fresh young women of Sinekli Bakkal came to sit with her in the evening. Fixing her eyes on Emine's, she said:

"Auntie Emine, Uncle Tevfik's friendship with the Gypsy Penbe is quite advanced these days."

She said, kindling her fire:

"With that pock-marked woman, that old hag of a dancing girl, with the worn-out face?"

The young woman scanned Emine's face. The long and bitter years passing over it had withered, yellowed it; her eyes from continual squinting had lost their luster. But the most fearsome place of this ugly and ruined face was the mouth. From smooth lips that clung tightly to one another, it had become only a thin line. A mouth like an old knife wound, covered over but still purple . . . Emine's young neighbor wondered what Tevfik had once seen to love in this repulsive face and said in a meaningful voice:

"These players are strange, Aunt. It is difficult to decide whom they will like. But nowadays if he should marry that pockmarked face, I would not be at all surprised."

When Emine was alone, she stirred up the brazier, she thought for a long time. Even after the coals were ash, she did not drop the tongs from her hand. The next morning, she went out to go shopping, but her feet brought her to Sinekli Bakkal Street and sticking her head inside the shop she looked around.

Tevfik had not gotten up yet, Rakim was making coffee in the kitchen. Rabia, having poured out on the bench the small change inside the tin box that Emine recalled very well, was counting it.

"What is this swagger, Miss Rabia?"

This voice made Rabia's face turn yellow like a corpse, and her eyes turned to Emine as if she saw a corpse.

"Why do look at me stiffly as if I were a snake? I think you didn't recognize me . . . If your father marries Penbe, you will come running back to the house of your mother ... But that time I will show you how many corners of the world there are."

"What is with you? Are *you* going to marry my father?"

"Don't make me laugh . . . Even if he howled like a dog on my doorstep, I wouldn't turn and look at him."

"Don't worry, after this my father would not even look you in the eye with his tail . . ."

"We shall see, Miss Rabia ..."

Emine put her head-covering back and left as soon as she had come. If a neighbor had heard her footsteps in the street, seen her there and told the Imam ... This would not have suited her business at all. But when she had turned the corner with utmost speed, she had the joy of victory inside. Rabia would certainly tell Tevfik that she had come to the shop, she would awaken his old weakness, he would loiter in front of her door ... Emine again would laugh ha-ha-ha . . . How sweet a vengeance this would be.

While Emine was putting together this beautiful dream, she didn't count on the intelligence of the dwarf Rakim, who was listening to the mother-daughter quarrel in the kitchen. As soon as Emine had gone, he ran to the kitchen and talked for a very long time with Rabia. More than anyone, he knew Tevfik's weakness. It was possibly dangerous to tell Tevfik that Emine had come to the shop. And Rabia did not tell her father about this strange visit of her mother.

Winter passed, Spring came. But no one who looked like Tevfik haunted Emine's doorway. She was more disagreeable, more persnickety, perhaps a little sick. Very often her breath was cut off, it took over the house of her soul like a cutting pain fixed there. Her head now looked completely like a corpse's head. Two old neighbors one day grabbed the Imam at the street corner. Whatever it might be, they didn't like Emine's color; they explained that it would be a good deed to make peace between the woman and her only child. The Imam muttering: "That's up to God!" turned his back on the women and went off. The women this time collared Tevfik at the door of his shop, broached the same subject to him. Tevfik's color disappeared, his lips trembled. In spite of all Rabia's objections, he sent her with the two old women to kiss Emine's hand.

Emine, prayer beads in her hand, her lips blue and purple, more than ever like one single old wound, was sitting shriveled up in the corner.

In spite of the fact that the weather was mild, there was a brazier before her. When she saw Rabia, she flew off of the cushion like a corpse rising from the grave. Her blue purple old wound mouth was opening. She rained down a shower of curses on Rabia's head with a vulgarity that was more pronounced than in the old days. Rabia, under the influence of this action and self-abasement in the presence of the neighbors, did not notice how wretched, how sick, her mother looked. The woman's wasted face, and in it the eyes sunken inside, did not awaken her mercy, but the trouble she had endured in the years of her childhood.

In the shop, to the face of her father as he walked up and down waiting for her with impatience, she bawled for the first time with anger:

"She does not want us . . . Did I not tell you?" And she began to cry sobbing and sobbing.

This was the last time the mother and daughter saw one another.

Chapter Thirteen

Selim Pasha's head gardener was sixty years old. But his back was still smooth, his body slender, his legs had preserved their old elasticity, his arms when they threw stones at a crow displayed the agility of a child, his feet trod on the earth as lightly as a tiger's. He walked on the street with the swagger of a grand vizier, in the garden he jumped around with the power of a twenty-year old. The skin of his face was sun burnt and wrinkled but behind white eyelashes the fire of his blue eyes had not yet died down, even his teeth were sharp and sparklingly white. He always clipped his white beard and mustache with care, keeping them small and short above his lips, and the expression of his upturned nose made him look like a bulldog. Under the red sash wrapped around him from his stomach to his armpits, his body was still like a whip-cord.

He had accumulated so much money that in his village near Manastir[29] he was reputed to be rich. Although he still loved with a jealous passion the garden that he had created by hand, at the same time he felt that he should train a successor that he could leave it to with confidence.

Because all of his own children were girls, he considered his nephew Bilal suitable for this task and the day that Bilal set foot in Istanbul he found him a job with Selim Pasha as the youngest manservant of the mansion.

Aside from small differences, this was a true fifteen-year-old copy of the Greek Bayram Aya. His legs which he had covered with short blue knee-breeches were a little more thin and nimble, his feet more like a tiger's, his body which he had wrapped up in a red sash was more tender, the long blue tassel of his red fez was let down with a more pronounced swagger. The same open blue eyes and white eye-lashes as his uncle, only the nose was different. Its tip was long, its nostrils open and twisted, his mouth was firmer and more stubborn...Instead of

---

[29] In Macedonia.

106

the brutality of a bulldog, his was the dominating profile of a falcon… Here you have it, as far as it goes.

The servants, citing his young age, at once tried to order him around. But he rebelled. He was haughty, fiery. He would dodge slaps and kicks like lightning, he would extricate his head and if he saw no other way out, he would climb a tree like a monkey, and proclaim to the hunters like a tiger cub snarling, "I'll show you!" And even elderly servants shied away from the eyes flashing behind his white eyelashes, they left him to his own devices.

One morning when the cook's apprentice, a fry pan in his hand, didn't find the water fountain in his own kitchen garden suitable, when he loitered lazily lazily, a boy of Bilal's age, Bilal chased him in the garden. When the boy escaped by jumping over the cherry laurels, he suddenly fell into the young roses. He came face to face with a tall man in a white skull cap and damask vest. Having come to the nursery only a minute ago after morning prayer to take the air and sniff the precious roses, Selim Pasha, when he saw the cook's apprentice with the fry pan in his hand and then Bilal who was thrown at his head like a ball, sputtered:

"What is this? What is this?"

At once the apprentice complained about Bilal's idleness and laziness: "And where did this boy appear from?"

"Your servant is the nephew of Bayram Aya, an apprentice gardener."

"Who are you?"

"Your servant is an apprentice to the head cook. The head cook wanted water, I said to the boy, 'Draw one or two buckets of water.' "

"Clear off, rascal, go and draw your own water for yourself!"

The apprentice cleared out. Selim Pasha scanned the child leaning against the wall, gnawing his fingernails from nervousness. He was pleased by the conceit of the blond head, the power of cold blue eyes in a red freckled face.

"Do you want to have a post that will make you a gardener?"

How could he not want that? He was saying to himself: "Now I will show all of them …"

"Tell your uncle, when the holiday is over, if he reminds me, I will inscribe you in the Galatasaray[30]."

This event saved Bilal completely from the servants' hazing. But when his work in the garden was finished, his heart was troubled, he would wander from street to street. He was looking for a friend for himself.

At once he began to loiter around the mass of children playing in Sinekli Bakkal. In his eyes, the big children did not want to receive him among them because they saw his desire and his capacity to be the head of every crowd he entered. They wanted to turn him off from the street which would mock his dress and his accent. But he, out of obstinacy, out of arrogance, every day would go to their leaders clenching his teeth and fists, saying: "I will show you!" From that time on, whenever he turned the corner of Sinekli Bakkal Street, all the children would come shouting: "I will show you!"

Bilal found out at that time the adventures of the Istanbul Grocery. One day when he was trying to spell out the sign-board's handwriting, his eye grazed the goods spread out before the shop. Panniers and panniers of sweet-waters, watermelons with red fleshed insides and rinds like emeralds, musk melons leaking honey from their slices, dried fruit arranged in the window … He wanted to take a goat horn and plunge inside. But all of a sudden the lady

---

[30] The Sultan's High School.

grocer passed to the door and chased flies away from the dried fruit with an enormous flyswatter in her hand, causing him to shy away and fall back. The girl had covered her hair with a piece of white muslin, but down her back half of the three brown pigtails were uncovered, and their tips shook at her waist.

The golden eyes with green spots of the girl grocer did not even look at Bilal . . . She was selling paper, pencils, gum erasers etc. to a troop of girls going to the school.

Her dress was no different from that of the school children, only her legs were long, her head in the air and more collected, more dominant over the outside world than anyone . . . She was speaking while her scrawny hands made up a packet with a speed that dazzled Bilal's eyes, meanwhile her eyebrows rose and her eyes grazed the boy with the foreign face and attire. In any event, the girl grocer made no gesture of welcome to the provincial child, who even after the children had gone remained rooted to the spot and was looking into her eyes. In a rough voice, she asked:

"Hey you, what's your name?'

"Bilal."

"Why do you look so very nastily at my face? Get in your carriage . . ."

Bilal went out to the street forcefully shaking his long arms, more ponderously and swaggeringly than ever.

With utter bitterness he was aware for the first time that his dress and speech were other than from Istanbul. Suddenly he hated Istanbul, he remembered Manastir like a holy land and he swore an oath to himself to show this arrogant city what the worth of Manastir was. This notwithstanding, he still loitered every day in the street that had given him such a bitter blow.

He and the grocery girl would look at one another as if they had declared war on each other, from one eye to another. Moreover, the two were unawares of each other's relations with the mansion.

The next evening, Rabia passed into the garden to get roses for Miss Sabiha, and she found Bilal in the nursery.

"What are you looking for here?"

And Bilal, trying to suck out the thorn that had plunged into his finger because of his confusion upon seeing Rabia, repeated the same question:

"What are *you* looking for?"

"Where is Bayram Aya? Mistress wants roses."

The grocery girl's speech, as if she belonged to the mansion, made Bayram Aya's nephew think. This couldn't be the girl hafiz that the servants had discussed with admiration?

He cut the roses, made a bouquet. Then he plucked a single yellow rose. His face like a beet from shyness, without having the courage to look at the girl, he extended the rose.

Rabia's first desire was to crush the rose under her foot, to throw it at Bilal's face. But she loved yellow roses so much that involuntarily she brought the rose that Bilal extended to her nose, sniffed . . . In a docile voice she said:

"If you come back to our street, pass by the shop . . . And I will give you sugar."

110

Chapter Fourteen

Tevfik set up his curtain in the Kabasakal Café and kindled his curtain candle. But the shadows that he reflected on the curtain made the spectators think as well as laugh.

The play was an old play, and he always began with a prayer, and finished with a prayer, for the life of the sultan. Moreover there was no outward change in the attire of the paper dolls. But he had changed their spirits. For example Profligate[31] was not that traditional stupid toff or little lord. His hangers-on took his money and did not make him look ridiculous. Tevfik's Profligate was capable and cunning. His money never gave out.

He was no different from Abdulhamid's ferocious big jobholders who lived off bribes, indeed he was not dissimilar to Zati Bey, onetime Prefect of Gallipoli, by then the Minister of the Interior. The paper doll playing the role of the Albanian was very reminiscent of the Head Gunsmith of the time. The dress, manners, and expressions were all old but the meanings were new. Only he would show this with such an artistic confusion and in the midst of the events so contrary to logic, that it was difficult to catch him and accuse him of making caricatures of this or that.

Tevfik brought examples of popular classes to life with an open and verisimilar expression. You heard the speeches of toadies who smile upon the great when they are before them, but mock and slander them behind their backs, a discourtesy born more of jealousy than righteous rebellion ... The people of Abdulhamid's period dwelt and spoke in much more negative places. The person of Karagöz himself became more lovely, more meaningful under Tevfik's hand. He too was a toady like all the others, like them a chatterbox. He soaked up with a grin the fist that descended on his head, the blow exploding in his ear, but his manner showed he was a practical philosopher of the people who wanted to explain that it was possible to act in a different way.

---

[31] Mirasyedi.

Tevfik had been persuaded by the constant insistence of the Kabasakal Café's habitués to do story-telling as well for two evenings every week. The strangeness of the historical legends that he represented rather than narrated spread from mouth to mouth. Again Tevfik became the most brilliant light of refined parties. Several writers who frequented the café proposed that he put on his stories as "plays". He refused. He insisted on making the characters that he had created speak differently each time according to his own imagination.

If Tevfik had been able to explain his purpose, he would have said that his intention was not expressible in the fixed script of an artist, but in life that changes at every moment. And if he had known the value of the thing called money, he could have become quite wealthy given this opportunity. But his earnings came to one hand and left from the other.

From then on, he had no time to take care of the shop. He had abandoned his work to Rakim and, when she had time, to Rabia. Three evenings he was at Kabasakal, mornings he spent in bed until noon, and after noon he would pass the time practicing his stories. Rakim and Rabia warmed themselves at the sun of Tevfik's newly resplendent prosperity and became more drunk than he was with his success.

And Rabia was growing up. It was not a growing up composed only of lengthening arms and legs, but a growing up of maturation and new strength, a difference that came from the ego. She preoccupied Sinekli Bakkal more than her father. A head taller than her contemporaries, she was a girl who walked with the dignity of a cypress, with an upright head and a bold glance that did not shrink from staring directly into the eyes of her interlocutors. When she came to the time of youth as a woman, she selected the dress of working women of the lower class. A long, loose-fitting black yeldirme, a white cotton head scarf that fell below her waist, and a veil that always was thrown down her back and never let down in front. For what working, retail saleslady would cover the face of her trade?

Her skin was burned like bronze from the sun, the old lines in her lovable mouth had been

112

completely and utterly effaced under the influence of her happy and full life, she had become a character who figured in the dreams of Sinekli Bakkal's rowdies. Although it was common for the rowdies to speak to the girls who had come to the age of marriage, to twirl their mustaches, even to pinch one who was by herself, there was not a single rowdy who had the courage to do these things to her. Her condition, half sacred because she was a hafiz, and her sharp tongue always ready with an answer, made men, whether young or old, respect her.

In the neighborhood, the crones who had the job of finding a husband for every girl of that age could not think of a fitting male for her. Men believed in marrying a doormat if they could. To the male universe of Sinekli Bakkal, the girl was a flag that recited publically. Moreover they could not find amongst themselves a single rowdy with the heart to be her mate.

In the days when Rabia was puzzling the intelligence of the neighborhood like a riddle, the Head Volunteer Firefighter Sabit Beyagabey gathered his gang to his side, and in a corner of the neighborhood coffee-house discussed the matter of Tevfik's daughter's marriage. Rabia seemed like a stain on the bravery of male wrestlers, like the masked Arab[32].

A mocking youth had just joined the group:

"You are the leader of the neighborhood bucks, Agabey . . . and you are a bachelor. It falls to you to bring this girl to heel. What other tough guy can break her obstinacy?"

Sabit Beyagabey spat into the hollows of his hands, kneaded them.

"I will show myself in the shop tomorrow, the other stuff is easy . . ." The youth smiled contemptuously:

"The other stuff, they all attained their desire . . ."

---

[32] Özengi, presumably a traditional character in Turkish wrestling, much like the villains in WWWF.

The heads of neighborhood volunteer firefighting companies esteemed Sabit Beyagabey above all others. As soon as the Beyazit tower raised the flag, they turned to the street corner, red lanterns in their hands, as soon as they had raised the cry, the Sinekli Bakkal company put red singlets over their heads, put their peasant clogs on their feet, raised the pump on their shoulders, and strode behind Sabit Beyagabey's black horse. Its cries drowned out the cries of the other teams like cat's meows, without doubt their nimble legs would carry them first to the site of the fire. In general, when people are such rough and ready fellows in their organiza-tions, they also have unsuitable qualities. But in compensation, being handsome fellows in their organizations, they also possess measures of peculiar manliness and virtue. The lords of the cry: "Very windy place … a life-threatening fire" very often are interconnected by the moral organization of the teams.

In one of the hours after noon when Sinekli Bakkal was deserted, a few young bloods began to stroll about. Sabit Beyagabey parted from their side, plunged into the Istanbul Grocery.

Rabia was alone. At Sabit Beyagabey, who was richly dressed up, having tidied himself up especially to pay her a visit, she did not even glance. However he, having pushed his small black fez farther back to show the place of an old wound remaining on his brow from his adventures as a rowdy, having extended more ostentatiously on his shoulders the tip of the silk handkerchief tied around it, having distorted his mouth in the rictus of one who gives a cry, he held his arms by his side angled out like pitcher ears and walked about with a more swaggering air.

His spirit was embarrassed by Rabia's indifference. The first thing he did was to seek the middle of the shop. He gave a little cough. But the girl, whose eyes were fixed on a notebook open in front of her, appeared not to hear. He turned his head, he let fly a wad of spittle two meters from under his armpit, and wiped his long mustache with his sleeve.

"Sister Rabia, look at me, listen to me."

"I am not blind, therefore I see; I am not deaf, therefore I hear."

"Do you know who I am? What I have done to men . . ."

"Do I see, do I see who you are? The Head Firefighter! What you have done to men? Your sister yesterday came to the shop, walking about with a bandage because you broke her arm. What more should I see you do? You frighten the girls at the fountain head, you also step on puppies . . . What else should I see you do?"

The green flames in her golden eyes wandered over Sabit Beyagabey's face. Was this still the girl who yesterday strolled down the street shaking her pig-tails? How could he face his gang if he was beaten by this girl? He distorted his mouth a little more, and began to try to speak in a fearsome voice:

"I make a morsel of men and swallow them, to me famous men ..." but he did not finish. Rabia flew at him:

"Is that so? Well I am not a morsel for your mouth. You are a bogey man of puppies, a cowardly bully. Look there is no one around. Let's see what you are going to do to me? Take this . . . tu tu tu tuuuu ..."

Sabit Beyagabey was really afraid. If Rabia should repeat her cry, when the neighborhood saw him alone they would think he had come to annoy the little girl, whereas his purpose was only a little bragging. Stammeringly he tried to calm the girl:

"Sister Rabia, I did not come to annoy you . . . I would be a dog if such a thing had passed across my mind. I am too uncouth to touch the hem of your skirt, I swear to God it's true!"

He so wanted to persuade Rabia, he so wanted to prove to her his courage but when he began to say the Fireman's oath "To the front of a windy, life-threatening fire" she was infuriated beyond all endurance. While she was looking for something in the shop to throw at his head, she was shouting:

"Silence, dog, piss off, animal, do I need your protection? Can I not tell dogs like you where to get off?"

The girl was almost rabid. Master Sabit this time found retreat, even a precipitate retreat, completely suitable to his bravado. He ran out of breath to the street corner, and with the command "Come on, let's go to the other street!" he dragged everyone to the gate of Selim Pasha's mansion, where he paused and began to say with a most portentous attitude:

"In this neighborhood there is no man worthy of wiping Sister Rabia's shoe." And he finished by saying: "Whoever shall look at her sideways, I will break his bones, I will make his mother cry." The young men each let fly a wad of spittle to a distance of two meters from their armpits, and wiped their mustaches on their lordly cuffs. "Long may you live, and when you go to the fire shout every shout in front of the shop," they said.

Sabit Beyagabey said agitatedly: "No, no, when we pass in front of the shop, we will be silent as mice . . . you understand?" They understood. From then on, when Sagit Beyagabey's team passed through Sinekli Bakkal Street, no one looked to the left or right, or bumped his neighbor's shoulder.

Chapter Fifteen

While the new star of Interior Minister Zati Bey was beginning to shine, it happened that Selim Pasha's was setting. He was still the Sultan's loyal slave, and he still crushed with the old vigor the Sultan's enemies, but he neither saw compliments from the Sultan, nor were fat red satin moneybags pressed into his hand. The splendor of the mansion could not be continued on his salary. One by one he was selling off the caravansaries, baths, shops that had been left to him by his ancestors, whatever was left, and he was reducing the household expenses.

In his position as Minister of Justice, it was still easy for him to make money from somewhere else. But he had his own personal standard of integrity. His connection with the sultan was legitimate, because to say nation was to say the sultan, he rewarded legitimate servants as he wished. Bribery was a treachery, a theft from the national pocket. Those who proposed bribery to him at this juncture regretted it to the end of their days.

During these troubled days, Pasha explained that the memories of rulers as of nations was short. Saying it was his duty, he continued in his service to the Sultan like a sheep dog. But he was very wretched, he would come every evening to Miss Sabiha's room to forget himself, he was diverted most of all by Rabia's presence, and he would listen to her gossip about Sinekli Bakkal. This evening he raised his thick eyebrows. He said a little sarcastically:

"What would happen if you withdrew from the shop from now on, Sister?"

"Impossible. Tevfik has no interest in salesmanship, and who would look after the shop when Rakim was busy with stocking it and showing goods to customers?"

"Tevfik is earning enough for all of you to live on."

"True, but what he takes with one hand he spends with the other. . .   And   why   do   you want me to withdraw, Sir?"

Selim Pasha laughed inwardly. What should he say? How could he say that her adultness, her beauty was a danger because of the neighborhood rowdies? But to this girl, this could not be said. She had attained the power and equilibrium of a man in her rich voice, in her upright head. How different she was from the women Pasha was accustomed to see in the mansion, continually exhibiting and exploiting their sexuality. And yet her face and her heart had a caressing loveliness. Without smoothing gel, without rouge, without kohl, without charcoal! Her tightly plaited hair had a charm all its own. Her waist, narrow like a boy's, the imperceptible roundness of her chest and shoulders that hardly penetrated one's vision, all these things gave her the charm of a young wild rose. Pasha stroked his beard. He was a little hesitant.

"Some vagabond, shiftless people come to the shop . . . In this neighborhood, being a grocer is truly not a thing for a woman of your age and face," he said.

"My mother was a grocer at a young age, Goodwife Zarafet sells dolma in Aksaray . . . "

"She is old and an Arab."

"In Beyazit courtyard there is a woman who sells prayer-beads, both younger and whiter than I am."

Miss Sabiha jumped in: "For goodness sake! Pasha . . . I would like to see the tramps who get the better of Rabia!"

Rabia told laughing the adventure of Sabit Beyagabey, who had passed by two days earlier. This amused Mistress very much, but Pasha again knitted his brows.

In him worry, approval, rebellion all mixed with each other. His religion and his sex forced him to defend women. It worried his heart that a woman as big as his hand should take on a male responsibility.

"You should have a proper man above you. It is their responsibility to protect you until the Imam marries you. Where is your father when a dog or jackal comes into the shop?" After pausing a little, he smiled and said:

"At any rate, from now on Sabit Beyagabey's team will behave responsibly in Sinekli

Bakkal. But nevertheless the time is coming when you will be married."

Rabia laughed, wrinkling the top of her nose: "As if I do not think about this! But who would take a girl dressed like a piece of underbrush, scrawny like me?"

"You will see if Tevfik gets married!"

"That clearly will not come about. Aunt Penbe's intention is corrupt, but if she casts her eye on my father, I have said bluntly that I will pluck it out. She no longer casts burning love-sick glances at Tevfik."

Miss Sabiha yawned: "For goodness sake, Pasha, you want to marry everyone off, and if Rabia gets a husband, who will amuse me in the evenings?"

This conversation made Rabia think deeply. Certainly she was informed of her own growing-up. But events that showed the sensitivity of her environment regarding this growing began to multiply.

It coincided that Rabia from now on continued her music lessons in Hilmi's room as a form of concert, and that Tevfik was free on Thursday evenings. Hilmi and his friends seemed to get used to Turkish music. Peregrini would play the piano for them occasionally. When he played, of course Rabia would lean on the piano and listen. It was becoming as natural for the pianist to see her there, as any other object he saw in the room.

This evening when his eyes suddenly glanced at Rabia, almost without seeing her, he became aware of how that head, which had barely reached the piano four years ago, now observed the room over the piano, and he trembled as if he had discovered an unexpected emotion, and his fingers stopped.

When Rabia saw the change in the pianist's eyes, her cheeks also blushed, the color of some ancient rare wine, and she let down her long eyelashes over her radiant eyes. Having understood that Peregrini had suddenly noticed she had grown up, had become a woman, she felt the strange shame that Adam felt in the garden of Eden when he first saw that he was naked. For the first time, the simple and casual relationship that had existed between them for years became a vineyard that was a violent beating to their hearts.

The pianist placed his hands on his knees. The result was that he felt inside like a sinner who enters a temple with dirty feet. He sought out Vehbi Dede with his eyes. He found him standing behind him.

"I noticed our child, your artist, how she had grown up, and I was a little confused," he said.

This event made manifest the question that was on all of their minds, Rabia's growing up. Hilmi was sad and lisped more than ever.

"I do not even want to think of the day when Sister Rabia is not in our midst. What bad customs[33] we have!"

---

[33] Adet means both customs and menstrual period.

The dwarf Rakim said, clinging to Rabia's skirt"

"In any event, she cannot flee from me. I am her uncle."

The meaning behind Rakim's joy, his triumph, -- his dwarfism, his abnormality – touched Rabia's heart. She stroked Rakim's shoulders absent mindedly. That evening, Rabia was thinking, and the life of a grown up was troubling and confusing her face. It was difficult to break away from a milieu she had gotten used to and loved so much. But why was she embarrassed? She was going to see Hilmi whom she loved like a brother in Miss Sabiha's room. There was no question of shunning Vehbi Dede, there was no woman who fled from him. The presence or the absence of Shevki or Galip to her was indifferent . . . In that case?

Her voice rose like someone reciting publicly to the world, saying:

"How many migrations there are, to the rich! I am a wretch of a poor tradeswoman, I see the male world in the mosque, why should I flee from Mr. Hilmi's friends?"

Tevfik took a deep breath. That the girl should shun men burdened him with the responsibility of taking a decision. But there was nothing that annoyed him enough to make him decide anything. Basically until now he had himself not taken any decision or made any choice. If it came to that, let the child shun men when she wanted!

After this evening, sometimes Rabia's mind was very full of Peregrini. For years she had been accustomed to him, connected to him. He was totally different from the others, he was a much more vital human being. His ugly face, changing with the speed of lightning, his black eyes that pierced the face of human beings and looked inside, the passing of the motley lines on his face from quietude to fiery emotion … All these things were peculiar to him. But, more than anything, Rabia was sensible to his hands. They were like two creatures that were different life forms from his own head… Two hands with hard, wrinkled, stubby fingers … As if they possessed a terrible secret, Rabia both balked at them and their movement made her heart beat convulsively. In those days when her mind was full of all these things, she asked Miss Sabiha a puzzling question:

"Mistress, is it possible for a Moslem girl to marry a Christian?"

"What a strange question, my child. It is an impossible thing. Because their marriage cannot be performed, because Sharia cannot be abandoned."

"But if they do not obey Sharia, if they are married . . . "
"The neighbors would stone both of them."

"But are there not Moslem men who take Christian wives?"

"Men are different. Did you not know that much?"

122

Chapter Sixteen

It was Hidirellez[34] day. Today there was not a single city under the sky that swarmed with so merry a crowd and not a single street that was the source of such a hubbub, mingling and confounding different sounds with each other, whose inhabitants would roast so much lamb and bake so much halva.

Tevfik turned very lazily in his bed. He was thinking of the gypsy Penbe shaking her black navel, in a paper house, now in the middle of heaps and heaps of people gathered in green meadows, among sounds of zurnas, tambourines, bell tongs and the clay drum.[35] After lunch he again stretched out in his bed and decided to rest up until mid afternoon. Only then did the toy makers' clackers[36] that brought the crowd to a frenzy pause and the crowd's hubbub lessened. At that time he would rise, roast the lamb, cook the pilaf. Vehbi Dede and Peregrini were invited to dinner.

The sun went down; the guests arrived. Rabia was in the kitchen with her sleeves rolled up and her skirts around her waist, helping Tevfik. The guests had taken their places in the garden under the grape vine. Single almond or plum blossoms dressed like brides would fly in at the open door of the kitchen, Peregrini and Vehbi Dede were heard chatting and laughing.

This evening for the first time, in the presence of these men who were so familiar, Rabia felt herself estranged and alone. They seemed to Rabia like men who go and turn a street corner opposite the path that she herself had just embarked upon, whom in a moment she would never see or hear. The friendship with them that years had produced was suddenly broken.

---

[34] May 6, the beginning of Summer.
[35] Zuma is a raucous double reed woodwind. Tef, zilli masha and darbuka are the names of the other instruments in Turkish.
[36] Kaynanazirilti, literally "mother-in-law racket", a rattle with a ratchet wheel.

123

This evening youth and custom were trying the gate of her heart. An almond blossom flying from the garden clung to her cheek.

Vehbi Dede was saying: "What do you say, Peregrini? Is not our music happy? Who said that?"

Afterwards, Rabia heard Dede striking the beat with his two hands and singing: "Spring blew me joy."

"How is this a Spring song, my friend? It is like a funeral march ... Listen to me, this is one of the songs they sing in Venetian gondolas . . ."

The pianist's voice sang a fast-moving, happy air. Only when he repeated the song did Rabia forget her loneliness a little.

Peregrini was silenced by the rattle of clogs over gravel as the girl brought coffee to the guests with the tin coffee tray in her hand. The apparition of a youth in the shadow of the grape vine reminded Dede of the lines of Vasif: "Let me look for a playmate of fifteen, a playmate of fifteen, a playmate of fifteen . . ." He was uniformed in the Galatasaray way, blue eyed, white eye-browed, freckled ... The cups on the tray shook, danced, and Rakim said: "Rabia, if you spill the coffee. . . "

And Rabia spilled the coffee. Peregrini, with a red silk handkerchief he took out of his pocket, holding Rabia's cotton robe over his knees, wiped up the coffee that had spilled on it; Rakim caught the tray and was bringing it to Dede, who moved not one whit from his place ... And from shame Rabia's young cheeks again had taken on the color of a rare old wine.

Tevfik came out of the kitchen. One by one with a match he took out of his pocket he lit the orange colored paper lanterns suspended from the arbor.

"The lamb is ready, gentlemen."

A moon as white as tin on the hilltops in the blue and purple sky, under which they chewed the lamb roast and pilaf slowly and thoroughly, with the seriousness of a religious ceremony. Rakim's mouth smacked with such gusto that …   With difficulty Rabia controlled her nerves until the end of the meal, she finished before everyone else and started to carry the plates out to the kitchen.

Rakim was going to the kitchen continuously, wanting to help Rabia with the dirty dishes. The mind's eye of the girl was seeing him as he ate the lamb in the orange light. What did a dwarf, a creature, have to do with a moon, round as a tray, suspended in the sky in Spring evenings? Rabia at first sulked, then snapped at him, at last put the coffee tray in his hand and sent him back to the garden. And he, like a dog driven away, let his shoulders sag and his head droop, with his eyes sadly sunken in their sockets, and very slowly joined the guests on the rush mats.

With one accord, three people were stretched out on the broad mat, their heads on their elbows, smoking cigarettes in their hands, while Rakim sat in the middle keeping one knee vertical, smoke leaving their nostrils in a constant stream. The huge head with a huge turban was turning from time to time to the kitchen, and then the smoke flew thicker and faster from his mouth. To Peregrini this evening the dwarf seemed a vision of suffering genius. Why had that spoiled girl snapped at the wretch this evening?

Behind the wall, in the neighboring gardens, other people also ate and smoked, a man coughed, a child wailed, a woman scolded her husband who had stayed too late. In the air, there was a sharp scent of earth that had just been watered. Every garden is watered in evening, thus it smells, but on Spring evenings there are also other smells: the scents of frying olive oil, yoghurt and cucumber mixed with garlic, jasmine, honeysuckle!

Remotely, from a far distant place, a humming comes from the street. There the climate is altogether different, in the street and in the garden the same man lives quite differently, thinks quite differently . . .

"Tak, tak, tak . . ."

A knocking at the gate. Rabia pulls the string and her voice calls out to the shop: "Who is that?"

"It is I ..."

A single red rose behind her ears, shaking a hand-painted scarf down her back, singing a gypsy song, Penbe was returning from the Hidrellez festivities. She did not offer to help Rabia when she came from the kitchen.

"There are guests in the garden, Aunt Penbe."

Penbe as if she didn't hear hastily went to the garden, laughing constantly and singing happy folk songs . . .

Again:

"Tak, tak, tak ..."

Again Rabia pulled the string, called into the shop: "Who is that?"

No answer ...

Rabia went into the shop, looked out the open door. The street was a water color painted in three colors, the sky was a deep eggplant seen through the eaves, the moon white, the houses black.

The yellow dog in front of the gate was wagging its tail and extending its nose into the shop.

"Was it you knocking at the gate, Sarman?"

She heard a cough behind the gate, a shy nervous cough. She bent down, saw a narrow shadow clinging to the wall, an uneven male voice that was still breaking said:

"It'me . . ."

"Me? And who's me?

"Me is Bilal! Master Hilmi sends his greetings, he summons Mister Tevfik and his guests to the mansion."

"Very well, now I'll say … you, you are Bilal, then!"

"And you are Miss Rabia, then. . . how much you have grown!"

The shadow sought Rabia's eyes. The girl noticed that his old clumsiness and fear had left him. She came to the threshold.

"Let me see, let me see . . . What beautiful clothes!"

Her red hands still wet and smelling of soap counted the yellow ribbons around Bilal's neck.

"Rabia, who has come?"

Tevfik was speaking from inside.

Rabia returned to the kitchen: "Master Hilmi wants us to come to the mansion," she said.

But she herself would not go. Her head was hurting, when she finished her work she would go to bed. They did not insist. The old people went away. The chasm between them and young Rabia this evening appeared so deep and dark that nothing could bridge it. But when she had finished her work, with a strange feeling she again went to the gate of the shop, opened it, looked out on the street. The delicate shadow was still in his place, he bent to the face of the white veiled girl, he sought the eyes of the girl with eyes wide open.

"What are you doing here, Bilal?"

"What are you doing all alone inside?"

"I was cleaning the kitchen. The garden smells nice. The weather is so warm that . . ."

It was not an open invitation, but nevertheless Bilal entered the shop behind the girl. They passed slowly and weightily through the shop and the kitchen and sat facing one another on the rush mat. From now on, they hid their eyes from each other. The two wanted to chat, but they could not find the idle words to say . . . Sometimes they raised their heads and looked at the moon, wanting to hide from one another the beating of their hearts acting like the anvil of an iron-worker in their chests. Rabia saw Bilal's narrow school jacket shaking like a bellows, and all of a sudden Bilal got up, and in front of the girl again passed slowly and weightily through the kitchen and shop. They stopped at the gate. Rabia first counted the yellow ribbons on his sleeves, then those on his collar, touching her fingers to Bilal's chin. She was ice cold and shivered a little.

Bilal's lips touched her fingers and lingered there a little . . . Rabia said in a hoarse voice:

"Last week I saw you at the mansion when you came from school."

When she was alone, she put out the gas lights and dragged her feet up the stairs.

Heavily she fell on her thin mattress. She could not sleep, a little later she got up. While she was thinking, her eyes on the ceiling, two rough wrinkled hands with stubby fingers caught her by the shoulders. Her lips were filled with something hot. This was a dream, but her taut body loosened and she fell into a dreamless sleep.

Chapter Seventeen

One week later Miss Sabiha said:

"Rabia, good fortune has come to you, Pasha will speak with Tevfik tomorrow." Under her breath, Rabia imitated the fortune telling bean of the Gypsy Penbe:
"Shall I have a Pasha ... shall I have a Bey?"

"I'm not joking. Sir Galip wants you. What's that face, monkey? Could you find anything better than him? His father is rich, there is neither a mother-in-law nor a sister- in-law, you will become the mistress of a household."

Rabia said with the face of a coat-hanger

"But I, I do not want a husband."

That evening, when Tevfik noticed the black circles around Rabia's eyes, he asked as he ate dinner in the garden:

"Are you sick, Rabia?"

"Sir Galip has wanted me, Pasha will talk to you tomorrow."

This time it was Tevfik's turn to hang his face up. There were different motives for the tears that burned their eyes, stirred up their hearts, for each other. That Rabia who alone warmed his eye and his heart should go and leave his house desolate . . . and also that she would leave Tevfik's class and go to an enormous mansion ... About all these things it was however incumbent on him to take a decision. As he scrutinized the girl's face with the tip of his eye, he asked:

"What would you say?"

She answered decisively. "I cannot become a mistress."

A light broke forth in Tevfik's face. O Satan! how quickly one decides things at that age. His eyes touched those of Rakim, scanning the two of them:

"What would you say, Sir Uncle?"

"I would say Sir Galip was a piece of fortune to be discarded thus, suddenly."

"That was nice. Uncle Dwarf, do you really want me to leave this house?"

"Don't act foolishly, Rabia. You are a girl without trousseau, without a dowry. You do not own an inn or bathhouse. You only have Uncle Dwarf . . . If you marry Galip, you will take me with you as your trousseau concubine. You will not find another husband like Galip, that you can stamp out in your matrix however you wish. Another might not even let me in the house."

"Fie, pig of a dwarf, fie. You see everything in your own interest!"

Tevfik gave Rakim's back a punch. But the three, having undergone the danger of separation, drew near each other like triplets. And this event created the first change in Rabia's circumstances in the mansion. When Galip and Shevki were there, from now on Rabia did not enter Hilmi's room.

.....

On Friday, Bilal went out in his school uniform to hoe up the rose shoots. Was it not there that he had had his first chance meeting with Rabia? Surely the girl would come there. He did not take off his uniform. The thin fingers of the girl had counted the ribbon on his collar, his sleeves and ... Her fingertips had touched his lips. The rising of the hair on his back that he underwent looked like his uncle if his uncle had once more had the power of a sixteen-year-old. He twisted his lip up, laughed like a snarl. Whoever had seen anyone hoe rose shoots in a school jacket?

The boy threw off his jacket, rolled up his sleeves. He began to hoe under his uncle's gaze.

He kept on hoeing, even after Bayram Aya left. From his ruddy freckled forehead over his long white neck, droplets of sweat were leaking, while his eyes longed for somebody among the shoots.

"Mistress desires roses."

Her voice was serious but her lips were laughing, there was that attractive crinkle in her nose. They cut the roses together, their fingers continually touching one another. Their happiness on that day was made up of that.

Bilal again was unable to speak, no matter how much he racked his brains. He was not able to find and say one single word. To her, Bilal was like a Spring day that comes and goes. She was glad of him because of his vigor, a little because of his wild beauty, and a little also because he was the first person in her life who had touched her.

After Rabia left, smelling the roses, Bilal felt despair that they were not successful. His infatuation with Rabia was not the emotion of a primitively physical youth. He was not crude and stupid as if he had paid no attention to Rabia. He had deep confused feelings that he did not yet know how to analyze.

In his mind Rabia was a sort of symbol of a ripe and mature city that both attracted and repelled him. He felt in his bones that the difference in her speech and appearance was the product of a lofty civilization that had taken centuries to be created.

That year Bilal, since he had tasted little of life in the school, had had little contact with the mystery called woman. He held a dominating position at the head of Greek, even of Bulgarian student groups. A few times, when strolling with students of his own age, he had become acquainted with Greek and Jewish prostitutes in Beyoglu. He had even gone once to the house of one of them. And this contact had produced very rigid opinions in him concerning women. For him there were two types of women: Beyoglu whores and family girls ... The former are obtained with money, the latter with marriage. Rabia belonged to the second category. For that reason, he had planned to get married to Rabia. One day he would take Rabia and show her what an astonishing man he had become ...

When they met on Friday's in the garden, he tried to explain to the girl that he was not an ordinary school student. While the nightingales twittered in the grove, while Spring flowers burned like white flame in the sun, he was trying to broach all the serious subjects. And the serious subjects were, according to Bilal, that he would own in the future horses, carriages, mansions, servants, courtesans ... The boy's heart was an internal combustion engine turning over with a crashing sound, his head was an underground munitions depot ready to blow ... His inner feeling of power, his desire of dominion was fiery enough to boil over and strangle outsiders . . . He did not doubt for a moment the wondrous deeds of his future. If he had been able to insert this conviction into Rabia's head ...

As far as Rabia was concerned, the feeling that she had composed for Bilal was a symptom of a passing natural impulse, the bond of a bird flitting from one tree to another. . . When her thin fingers --- it was becoming a custom for the two of them --- persisted in strolling along the boy's collar, she would touch his chin and stroke the golden fuzz that had lately appeared on his lips. But there was a side of Bilal that rebelled against this touch that brought him to his knees. He found Rabia flighty, inwardly he did not deem her behavior suitable to a "family girl", to a family girl that he would marry later on. He did not know that this freedom, this naturalness in Rabia came from innocence, from the fact that she had not been taught life's dangers from the time when she was strong enough to imagine them . . . In any case, as the boy's condition because of this had entered into an electrified state, he at once began to discuss the future with her. But this talk constricted Rabia's heart ... Because she had grown up among thoughtful and mature men whose careers were fixed. She only wanted to play with Bilal. Sometimes to interrupt Bilal's chatter she wanted to discuss Vehbi Dede or Peregrini. But Bilal would say with a sarcastic expression:

"Why should I talk about these musicians? Everyone who associates with Hilmi Bey and his friends is a fruit-cake."

"In that case, whom should I talk about? You alone?"

"About Selim Pasha ... Have you seen the man? He bastinadoes whomever he wants, he exiles at his discretion, he makes everybody's mother wail, no one can say a word. Look at any one of his mansions, look at his splendor ... I want to be like him. My wife like his will have jewels, carriages, horses ..."

Rabia at once interrupted this speech, because she didn't like the things he was attributing to Selim Pasha.

"Pasha is not at all the man you describe, some one who makes every one's mother wail, who bastinadoes the whole world. He is so courteous, so well-bred that ..."

"He seems that way in the harem. One of his defects is that he is not educated ... If he knew what I know, if he read a little French ..."

Bilal stopped talking here. He always saw himself as Justice Minister in the future. He would bastinado, he would exile, but he would act in a way that was more within the bounds of what national security required, more by the book. But Rabia said, with an expression on her face that insulted the intimacy of their first meeting:

"You want to be like Galiba, like Sabit Beyaghabey."

Here is tyranny and force, however much it is in the bounds of what is required, however much it appears as symbolic power, and to Rabia it seemed like a type of hooliganism. And to Rabia his showing that his desires were as brilliant as the swagger and braggadocio of a head fireman plunged into her heart like a needle. And then he balled up his fists, became beside himself, and gnashed his teeth as he said:

"One day I will show you who I am, Rabia."

They were discussing this whole topic in the garden on the last Friday of the Summer holiday. The meadows had finally faded, the leaves had yellowed, the nightingales had become quiet, the breeze had begun to blow very coldly.

Bilal, without explaining these big things that filled up his heart to overflowing, perhaps since for the first time he was in despair of the probability of ever explaining them, enfolded the girl in his powerful arms like a man attacking an enemy and for the first and last time kissed her on the lips.

As soon as Bilal's hot lips, covered with silken fuzz, had touched Rabia's mouth, it was as if the beak of a flying bird came into her heart, and her inside ached sweetly, sweetly. The green flames of her eyes glittered and glittered, she walked very quickly among the denuded branches and said to herself:

"I wonder what this boy finds to enjoy in speaking like Saltless Bekir in Karagöz, why he wants to make the all the mothers in the world wail?" she lamented.

....

The very frequent meetings of the two children in the garden during the Summer holiday did not escape the eyes of the servants. Although these encounters were not hidden, and the two had not sought out a secret corner like lovers, nevertheless a little gossip started up during the Sultan's procession. All the servants were convinced of the uprightness of the girl hafiz. It seemed to them that one who was only the nephew of the gardener was chasing after the girl to marry the hafiz girl whose place was under the eye of Pasha and Mistress and whose fame was legendary. How fortunate he would be if the boy had the girl's heart!

They placed this in the ear of Bayram Aya. They supposed that the old gardener would pull up his trouser legs and embrace Pasha's feet, to give Rabia to his nephew. However the business did not turn out thus. Bayram Aya pounded his fists on the ground, and immediately started frothing at the mouth. Had Bilal been born for the daughter of an orta oyunu player, a girl whose trade was being a grocer? Whoever spread this gossip, he would break his eye. The head gardener was from a country of "bucks", whereas they were all men who loved Anatolian boy servants, the effeminate and the speechless. Particularly as soon as they came to Istanbul, all men had become soft. In his coffee- room, no one continued this subject.

But Bayram Aya, in pondering what the servants had said, reflected. He had believed in Bilal's radiant future, he had trusted the boy as he trusted himself. It was the first sign of prosperity that Pasha had liked him and sent him to the school. Sometimes sons-in-law of pashas, grand viziers, had they all not come from men whose aptitude the pashas liked and whom they educated? Perhaps Pasha would want to marry the boy to his daughter, and perhaps later he would train him and leave his place to the boy! Mr. Hilmi was so bloodless, so lifeless ... Bilal was like fire. Perhaps Pasha had even talked about Bilal to the Sultan. Shall a Rabia now spoil all these sweet fancies?

136

That morning Selim Pasha picked the slugs one by one from the roses, dropped them on the ground, stepped on them, wrinkled his eyes and face as he crushed them. He would have been incapable of doing this, did he not love roses so much. He felt pain for animals; the man had never in his life slaughtered a chicken. To slaughter a soul, to cause pain -- these things were outside his compass, if they were outside his duty -- were matters that he abhorred.

Bayram Aya coughed to attract his attention: "Merhaba, Bayram Aya!"

"Merhaba, Pasha our Lord!"

"How's it going? It seems you want to say something?"

"Yes, Pasha our Lord. An affair of honor . . ."

The slug dropped from Pasha's hand, he forgot to step on it, his eyes erupted in fire. Such an expression of wrath covered his face, which had been mild a moment before, so that if Bayram Aya's heart had not been what it was he would have lifted his soles and fled.

"What do you mean to say, rascal?"

The gardener explained. Bilal and Rabia had met very often in the garden, the servants had noticed, the danger of cotton playing with fire had led Bayram Aya to worry …

Pasha took a breath. His face and his voice assumed an expression of mildness and politeness beyond the call of duty.

"Look at me, Bayram Aya. This is not so bad a thing. The two are equal to one another. Mistress will set up a house for Miss Rabia, and perhaps when the boy graduates from school I will find him a post …"

The gardener shook his head. In his opinion, Miss Rabia was in no way the equal of Bilal. She was a very excellent female religious and if it should come to pass, she was suitable to marry an Imam, a grocer, perhaps a master musician.

Pasha again kitted his brows. "Who is Bilal?"

Who indeed? The gardener explained. He was the child whose natural ability Pasha had noticed and whom he had taken in hand and sent to school. He had been kneaded from the dough that in time would become a vizir, a son-in-law to Sultans. Bilal at the very least could become the son-in-law of a Pasha. While the old gardener was explaining these things, bringing water from a thousand and one streams so as not to annoy Pasha, again Pasha's face became severe. He understood and he was not angry. This was the social democracy of the old Turkish assembly, in his opinion nobility was in the capacity of the individual. Only until now his mind had not been preoccupied with his daughter. Both older and weaker than Bilal, she was an unlovable girl. If anyone took her in marriage, it would be a needy young man who wanted to benefit from Pasha's position. He did not think his daughter was worthy of hand-some, fiery Bilal. Especially if Rabia whom he loved so much had contracted her heart to the boy … He again knitted his brows.

"If Bilal has enjoyed himself with Miss Rabia, I will break his bones. Alright if they only met in the garden, if the servants exaggerated the business. Does not Miss Rabia talk with everyone? But …"

Bayram Aya behaved agitatedly. He was convinced only a minute ago that there had been evil on both sides. If not, if not … Bayram Aya had a standard for weighing his reputation. And his standard was also a terribly extreme Rumelian[37] standard. If he believed that evil had come to pass, he would tear Bilal's flesh apart bit by bit with his own hands, even his own mother would not recognize her son.

---

[37] Rumelian refers to the Greek part of the Ottoman empire.

After Pasha said, "Let me think a little," he left the roses and the gardener and went to the harem. In his room, his mind was occupied with this business until evening.

That courageous, that intelligent, that lovable Rabia! If in her heart she had the least little affection for Bilal, he would definitely give them to each other. If not . . . At that time, he could not imagine Bilal as his son-in-law. The first right of selection belonged to Rabia.

In the evening he went to his wife's room. Both Rabia and the Gypsy Penbe were there. The girl was telling a few stories, both Miss Sabiha and Penbe were laughing. When Rabia saw Pasha, she dragged the cushion by the side of the divan where he always sat, and she brought his ashtray and matches.

Pasha looked with compassion and tenderness on the brown pig-tails shaking down her back, her swift movements, her beautiful eyes.

"Have you noticed how his school uniform suits Bilal, Rabia?"

"Yes. If a sultan saw him, he would give him his daughter in marriage."

Her voice was cross, bitter, sarcastic. That evening when she came to the mansion, she had crossed paths with the old gardener. Bayram Aya had nearly blocked her path, and discoursed about Bilal at great length. And in this conversation, the girl had discovered things that were very similar to Bilal. He talked about what a big man every boy of his would become. And without considering whether it was appropriate, he said that Bilal would become the son-in-law of a Pasha. The old man's voice was almost threatening, as he struggled to say: "Open your eyes, the boy is not your match." Rabia -- although unjustly -- made a decision against Bilal to connect this interview with Bilal's old words. Certainly the boy's talk of horses, carriages, servants and concubines had to come from a plan to become Selim Pasha's son-in-law.

Pasha noticed the tempest in the girl's face. He laughed.

"Certainly the boy is handsome enough to be a Sultan's son-in-law!"

Rabia also laughed, showing all her teeth. She snatched up Hilmi's fez, lying on a cushion, and put it on her head. She said what they had said with Bilal's swagger and accent. She began by showing everything to everyone, making everyone's mother wail, and at the very end she finished by expressing admiration for Selim Pasha.

Miss Sabiha was splitting her sides, but Pasha was not yet laughing. He knew how the new young men did not like him, even his own son. So in Galatasaray there was only one youth trying to take him for a model?

"Do you not like men of power and rank, Rabia? Why do you make fun of the boy, saying he has grand ambitions?"

Rabia shook her shoulders. Penbe began to mutter a song. "Sing it fast, Miss Penbe, it's a lively tune."

"He opened the window, the boy Bilal,
The pistol exploded,
I wonder, is Bilal bloody, whom has he crushed?
I'll not marry you, boy Bilal,
I'll not marry you.
Even if you pester me for six years, I still won't like you.

"Does Miss Penbe's song fit your mood, Rabia?" Rabia looked at Pasha and winked an eyelid. "Completely, Sir Pasha."

This song spread from the mansion like an epidemic. Penbe shook her navel with this air to divert Miss Sabiha.

Tevfik, as soon as he had learned this song from Penbe, began to sing it in Karagöz. The street children shouted out this song morning and evening in Sinekli Bakkal.

This song put Bilal's nerves into an evil state. His own pain caught up with him. Rabia couldn't look at his face for a reason she did not explain. And once his uncle took him aside, and spoke to him as if the promise had been given to Pasha's daughter, and it had become settled that he would become Pasha's son-in-law. At the end he said that if he saw him speaking to Rabia he would break all his bones.

He had no eyes for Pasha's ugly old daughter. His heart was still attached to Rabia. . . In spite of the fact that the girl did not speak to him, fled from him, on weekends he haunted Sinekli Bakkal like a ghost. Even once or twice he entered the shop with the pretext of buying something. But Rabia still did not look at his face. She said in an official voice: "Uncle Rakim, see if Bilal Effendi wants something," and went into the kitchen. After this, to take revenge on Rabia, his heart became content to be the son-in-law of Pasha.

One last evening yet, on a moon-lit evening, he came to the shop's gate. The memory of Hidrellez evening made his heart ache so much that he leaned his back against the gate, he didn't move. From the room over the shop he heard Rabia's rich voice:

"I will not marry you, boy Bilal, I will not marry you,
If you pester me for six years, I still won't like you."

141

Chapter Eighteen

Bilal's folk-song had come and gone from Sinekli Bakkal like an outbreak of fever, even his image faded from Rabia's memory.

Tevfik was sick, he had caught typhoid. They were saying it began with a fever. The mansion doctor came every day, gave him salts of sulfate and English salts and they sweated him in the evenings. Rabia did not leave her father's side, she never went to make the response that Ramadan. Hardly five coins came to the Imam's hand.

Like everything concerning Tevfik, his sickness became the main event of the neighborhood. In the last years, no one had died from a notable illness. There were childhood illnesses like rubella and scarlet fever and some old men. Only this lion-like young Tevfik, Istanbul's unique Karagöz and public story-teller, was bedridden in the neighborhood by such a famous illness. More than ever with some pride the women pointed out the grocery shop to strangers. This was an event that both showcased neighborhood solidarity and increased its fame.

The doctor had recommended quiet. Even the street paused. The children took their tops and balls and went to the other side of the neighborhood.

Every house and row house cooked a meal and brought it to Rabia, thank God no one was so poor that they couldn't cook some kind of soup, no one was so poor as to remain outside of this great drama. It was a drama where everyone was required to play a role of kindness and goodness, and everyone played his role with great simplicity and realism.

Rabia took care of Tevfik, Rakim of Rabia, and the Gypsy Penbe was there every day to help Rakim . . . When she cleaned the stairs, she heard Tevfik shouting and calling out in his sleep. It was all about Emine, about the days of his first youth . . . Once or twice he revisited the evenings when he amused Zati Bey in the Gallipoli gardens. At those times, Rabia felt twenty years older.

At last the illness ran its course, passed away. Tevfik was like a skeleton and, even in the period of his convalescence, didn't want Rabia to leave his sight. Miss Shükriye came every day with a food basket in her hand to ask after her in the name of Mistress.

"This evening you could certainly come; you could leave Mr. Tevfik with Penbe."

Rabia was making coffee for Miss Shükriye in the kitchen, and the woman was sitting opposite her on a tiny chair, her basket in front of her.

"This evening it is not possible ..."

"It is both Kandil-eve, and a henna evening. Miss Mihri is marrying Mr. Bilal. The wedding will be Thursday."

"At last the apprentice gardener has gotten to be the son-in-law."

"Why do you talk thus, my little Rabia? He has become such a handsome boy that ... Miss Mihri is still Miss Mihri. We have prepared a room for Mr. Bilal in the selamlik. Mr. Son-in-law is up, Mr. Son-in-law is down .... You should see his swagger!"

Miss Shükriye was not ignorant of the Rabia-Bilal adventure that had been bruited about. But in no way did she say these things to spite the girl. Rabia like herself was a girl of the poor working class. It was not necessary to beat around the bush or protect them in giving bad news. It was purely to gossip with Rabia that she was saying these things.

Rabia did not lift her eyes from the fire. It was not possible to tell from her closed face what she was thinking. In that head of hers, she was thinking of Mihri's crooked chin, her dull eyes, her pale badger lips ... especially her lips ... Bilal would kiss them as he had once kissed her own lips. A touch that would connect and flee like a bird's beak … Her heart ached.

"I cannot leave my father any more, Miss Shükriye, I kiss Mistress's skirts, do not be offended, my lamb."

She placed the dried fruit from the basket on a plate, she took hold with her hand of the glass from Miss Shükriye's hand. Very hastily she went upstairs.

Near evening, Dede and Peregrini came to inspect the invalid. Dede went upstairs, the pianist sat in the chair that Miss Shükriye had sat in, and tried to amuse the girl who was making another coffee. The child's eyes were abstracted, her face was pale.

"Shall you take your coffee upstairs?' she said.

"No. I will sit here a little longer." Rabia left his glass in front of him and picked up the tray. She took away Vehbi Dede's coffee.

As Peregrini stroked the cat Tekir who was stretched out by the brazier, he heard voices from the shop. Immediately after, Rakim plunged into the kitchen, his eyes worried:

"Yesterday evening, Rabia's mother died, Signor. How should I tell the girl?"

"If were still a priest, I would know."

"Uncle Rakim, Vehbi Dede wants the nargile. Leave the shop door open and come, when you are not here I will notice if a customer comes in."

She made ready the nargile, and gave it into Rakim's hand. Her cheeks were red, her eyes glistening.

Peregrini guessed that something new had happened to change the girl's face into a little bit of its previous withdrawn self.

"Tevfik is very happy. He made a joke with Vehbi Dede like his old self. When are you going to go up?"

Peregrini didn't answer. His eyes became moist with pity, and he looked into the girl's eyes. Perhaps there was something besides pity, perhaps he was showing the girl a feeling he had that he was not even aware of himself. At any rate, the girl was embarrassed, she lowered her eyelashes, she was looking at her hands lying on her knees. If a moment before the memory of Bilal had pained her heart so much, this strange look of Peregrini was giving her a different sweet pain. What did this mean?

When the pianist rose from his place, her heart began to beat powerfully. She covered her face with her hands because of a momentary fear.

The pianist came over, two calloused hands touched Rabia's shoulder, and then took the girl's hands from her face:

"Your mother has died, my child."

Rabia did not cry. Her eyes were bone dry, but there was something so bitter in the way she looked at the pianist that ... Why was she not crying? Why did she not say anything?
He, a very strong man, with difficulty himself was keeping back his tears. Why, why did he not dare to caress the shoulders of this girl who was growing up in his hands? At last Rabia opened her mouth:

"I wonder, will Tevfik die?"

"Why should he die? But you, in any event, conceal this black news until he is well. For you it is difficult, but … If you want to pour out your heart, talk with me, I know how to say mother, I too had a mother in my country …"

"Really?'

"And do you think old musicians are born without mothers?"

"You are not so old that…"

Why was he so pleased that Rabia did not find him old?

Rabia asked with a deep curiosity: "Did you never go to see your mother?"

Now the hand of this dangerous child was tearing at shrouds of ghosts that Peregrini had buried. How sweet it would to expound to her upon the past that he did not even talk about to himself. Evening had completely descended upon the kitchen. Everything was in shadow, the flames in the brazier were ruddy with a soft darkness, Tekir was quietly wheezing on the floor.

Rakim's head appeared through the door: "Vehbi Dede is calling for you," he said.

Chapter Nineteen

When she made Tevfik's bed and washed his hands and face, Rabia's accustomed merriment reappeared. But her father still noticed there were dark circles around her eyes.

"This Ramadam you didn't make a single response. I wonder what the Imam did? They say that the old man has become quite poor. Strange, I saw Emine in my dreams last night."

"Every night you see a different dream, enough with your dreams." She caressed her father's matted hair:

"This morning, Uncle Rakim will shave you, your beard and moustache are mixed up with one another, they say you have turned into a bogey man. No, noooo, it is not possible to kiss you, your beard gets on my nerves."

"Emine wanted to tell me something."

"Emine, Emine . . . Now shush let me see. Uncle, you put on the soap. I will hold his hands in case he doesn't behave."

"Are you jealous of your mother, sugar? I will persist in talking about her. Surely in the feast of the Sacrifice[38] you will go and kiss her hand, do you understand?"

Afterwards, very distractedly, he was saying: "I wonder what she was trying to tell me? I do not remember anything."

"Should I take the soap bowl, Uncle?"

---

[38] Eid al-Adha, on the tenth day of the last month of the Islamic calendar, when Moslems celebrate the willingness of Abraham to sacrifice his son Ishmael. It comes about 70 days after the end of Ramadan.

Tevfik was listening to sounds of "Allah is great" coming from the street. "A funeral is passing, Rabia, look out the window, is it a woman or man?"

Rabia kept her face stuck to the glass. Was the woman within this coffin covered in shawls the one you gave her no peace and comfort for so many years? On top was pink silk crepe, perhaps crepe she had put on to seem pleasing to Tevfik. The Imam had on his head the most enormous turban, on his back a cavernous black Ottoman overcoat... How bone dry he was, like a match stick. Beside him there were several other old turbaned Imams like him. not a crowded funeral ... The coffin was born on the collapsed shoulders of several wretched men reading the Koran. Rabia hunched over, face down, sobbing, and whimpered hoarsely:

"Only don't you die, Tevfik, only don't you die."

The invalid smiled. An anxious expression passed over his face.

"Of which I was so afraid. Certainly it is a man's funeral; don't worry, my Rabia, while you are alive I shall not die."

That day in the afternoon he slept for a very long time. Rabia was in the kitchen, putting in order the accounts, which she had neglected for a very long time. Rakim was wandering up and down in the shop, looking at the tired expression on her wretched pinched face.

A stranger wearing a long red fez and with hyena eyes entered the shop. The girl grocer lifted her head, looked at him. Then as if she had not seen him she licked the lead pencil and began to write.

The strange customer stared about himself with anger at being neglected. Rakim opened his eyes in fear and remained frozen in one spot. But quickly he recovered himself. He began to hover around the customer. The man with the bug eyes looked at the dwarf crawling under his feet as if he was a worm:

"Is this Tevfik's shop?"

"Yes sir, yes sir."

This popeyed swaggering rascal and Rakim's fearful glances were getting on Rabia's nerves. She asked in a very disagreeable voice: "What do you want?"

The stranger did not condescend to answer the girl, but ordered the dwarf: "Tell him to come here."

"I will go, I will give him the news. He is sleeping."

"Woe on the soul of her father! Is the rascal a grocer or a pasha?"

"He was sick, sir. If you want, I'll bring you beside him."

"What, what? Shall I have to attend upon his majesty?"

He contracted his eyes, bent his neck, like a rabid bull preparing to attack:

"You, do you know whom you're talking to, rascal? I come on behalf of Zati Bey."

"My father knows Zati Bey."

"Thus you are Miss Big Sister?"

He twisted his mustache, stared at the girl with obscene eyes.

"You are a dog of a rowdy, you . . . who do you think you are?"

The stranger retreated a little, turning to the dwarf:

"This Miss Big Sister, does she in fact know who Zati Bey is?"

"Like yourself, brother. The illness of her father has confused her, pardon her fault."

"Really, brother! You scrofulous son of a bitch, you . . . Let's go, come along with me!"

Rakim in front, the stranger in back, they went upstairs. There was the weight of impending disaster in the air.

From the shop door came a hoarse voice, asking: "Sister Rabia, are you alone?"

"Ah . . . you are . . . Sabit Beyaghabey?" Rabia, quite pleased, took heart: "Do you want something?"

"That Nimrod, the son of a pig, swine, was asking for the shop. He left his carriage at the corner. I came to see if anything was needed. Birds don't fly in the street, the crowd has left … The damnable fez of that dog of a rascal has frightened everyone."

"Do you know who he is, Aghabey?"

"I understood who he was from his fez. What did he ask for here?"

Rabia had at last understood. She had heard that long red fezes were the insignia of detectives. But she had forgotten because she had not such a man in Sinekli Bakkal.

"Zati Bey has summoned my father."

150

"To his family tree's grave . . . For your religion, for your faith . . ."

"He is not influenced by religion." And as she spoke, she suddenly brought her hand to her mouth and made a sign.

Footfalls were coming from the staircase. Aghabey now leaned on the counter: "An oke of soap, an oke of soap . . ."

He was ordering the first thing that came to mind.

Tevfik, walking unsteadily between Rakim and the pop-eyed stranger, came into the shop:

"I'll be back in the evening, Rabia, don't worry, it must be a mistake," he said, trying to satisfy the girl.

The detective pulled on his sleeve, and they passed into the street with Rakim behind them.

Rabia and Sabit Beyaghabey remained in front of the door until the sounds of wheels had been cut off. Afterwards, they put out their heads, looked in the street. Truly birds were not flying, the crowd was not passing. "The red fez" blew like an ill wind in Sinekli Bakkal, it had herded the poor inside under its droplets.

Chapter Twenty

For the tenth time, the Interior Minister read the journal in front of him

He began by saying: "Their weaknesses, the Sinekli Bakkal Imam . . . owing to his religiosity and devotion," and after examining and classifying this classic journal in his mind, with a red pencil held in his hand he underlined points when they were useful to his task, and wrote several things as well on a blank sheet of paper.

Which were the most powerful points that he could use against his old rival, Selim Pasha? Pasha was hurting the people, he was oppressing the Islamic community . . . Poof, this was no concern either of the sultan or of Zati Bey. Pasha's son was said to be a Young Turk, he would gather in the evening with his friends and organize depravity and sedition... This was a point to consider ... He immediate passed the red pencil underneath. "Without fearing God, with no respect for the Prophet, behind the power and position that our angel-tempered Lord has granted, he conceals his expertise in depravity from this reasonable person . . . He drew two lines under this.

The part of the journal concerning Selim Pasha's mansion was quite diverting for Zati Bey. His wife was said to be a lesbian, a witch who had cast a spell to make her husband seem charming to the Sultan . . . Very well, these lines got one line each. The sultan was very nervous about this type of secret powers. If it was not like Ebulhüda and his gang, why would you gather together a group of beggars to make amulets, incantations, breathing spells?

"What is this, what is this?" Now the journal was discussing a blonde concubine named Kanarya. It said this dancing girl had been given to the Palace. The purpose being through her to influence the Sultan from near by. The girl was equipped with tricks and stratagems altogether peculiar to the female gender . . . The red pencil hovered in the air. This was a point where Zati Bey was quite weak.

As he read, the Interior Minister found the position of Selim Pasha in this convoluted journal a little bit of the second rank, even an accidental insinuation into the journal. It was understood that the main preoccupation of the Imam was to bring Tevfik down. He characterized him as a vulgarian who, after his return from exile, had corrupted the general moral tone and defiled our land.

In truth, if the causes impelling the Imam to write a journal about his ex son-in-law could not be said to be lawful, they could be called human. When the money from Rabia had been cut off, he had suffered extreme poverty. Besides this, Emine's death in sickness and destitution ... And her curses toward Tevfik until the last breath of her life had overturned the Imam's essentially distraught reason and had fanned his grudge toward Tevfik. At the same time, still without at last planning for himself, he had applied to Pasha, had explained his condition.

Pasha, being occupied with his own troubles in those days, had suddenly said, rather coarsely:

"If you don't want to sponge on a small child to the end of your life, look to your own head for a plan!" and with an expression drove the Imam back away from him. And it was only at that time that Mr. Hadji Ilhami saw in the list about Tevfik an opportunity to take vengeance on Selim Pasha. At that time it was widely known among the people that Selim Pasha's star had set, and Zati Bey's star was shining with a great power. Who knows, perhaps thus with a journal he could have also been courting Zati Bey's favor.

After Zati Bey had taken down short anecdotes about Selim Pasha, he began to read the parts concerning Tevfik with more care.

Tevfik was Selim Pasha's man, Hilmi and his gang congregated in the room above the shop ...

It was not worth reading this. Tevfik, when he did public story-telling performances in the Kabasakal Café, was said to have told an entirely new version of the story of the "Profligate". It was said by everyone that this new "Profligate" was Zati Bey. He had created the crowded stages called "luxury in the Gallipoli gardens" so that ...

Zati Bey did not like this. He decided to destroy Tevfik absolutely. But how? He was ready to sacrifice ten years of his life to become a vizir provided with the power to have hung or strangled whomever he chose, as happened in the time of the old sultans. But this was now not possible.

He drank two coffees, smoked ten cigarettes. For nothing, he would exile the rascal to whatever place he wanted! All right, but in the provinces how many governors had fixed their eyes on the Ministry of the Interior ... If Tevfik met with one of these ... No, no ... The most legal way was to scare Tevfik, forbid him from performing his art ... Even possibly to use Tevfik to investigate Selim Pasha's mansion and his son more closely. This was a more political course of action, a measure more becoming to an astute man like Zati Bey. And that was the very decision he had taken after dispatching the civil servant Zazir Bey to bring Tevfik in.

Tevfik barely managed to haul himself up three flights of stairs by clutching the banister. His knees were shaking, his eyes were clouding over, he almost passed out from fear. But at the same time his eyes were noticing in detail the difference in Zati Bey's new house. This was a very different house from the house in Gallipoli, with its empty clutter and borrowed furniture. Everywhere was full of gilded full-length mirrors, consoles and tables. The furniture was jam packed, crowded on top of itself, whether it was appropriate or not. The rascal seemed to have conveyed to his house almost every Beyoghlu shop. Moreover on the walls there was a series of Zati Bey's, in uniform, out of uniform, painted and unpainted. The house of that époque's nouveau riche aping the European style ... Where was Selim Pasha's honest tasteful house that depended on light, openness, simplicity? Even the room that Zati Bey had furnished and adorned in imitation of a so-called "Old Turkish Room" was like a corner of the antiquarian Hayim's shop.

The house's servants, like the chattels and their arrangement, were imitations as well ... Without being needed, there was one crowd on top of another. They goose-stepped in place in front of Tevfik, behind him, up and down. Some stood on the stairs racing their chins with each other, some laughingly without meaning or sense tried to serve Tevfik, some were insolent and spoiled!

As the ears of a musician would have been pained to hear the false notes made by an untrained orchestra, thus Tevfik's honest natural taste heard with misery the falsehoods in the harmony of this imitation man and his furniture.

As he entered Zati Bey's presence, he found the same incongruence in the dress and manner of his old patron. The old Zati Bey's collar was wrinkled and dirty, the buttons of his jacket seldom fastened, his fez always a little thrown back, he was a man whose expression was free and easy and rather coarse. Now, behind his new dress and his new tidy air, pieces of the old Zati Bey were peaking out, but the new Zati Bey was not yet a completely fixed personage.

His official jacket very tightly buttoned up, his boots shining, his shirt sleeves more shining still, his sleeve buttons diamonds . . .

To Tevfik, this new Zati like his furniture and his house gave the impression of an actor coming on to play a role but not skillfully.

He made a place for Tevfik facing himself. Insinuating with all his might how lofty, how noble an act it was for a great man preoccupied with affairs of state to converse with a contemptible creature like Tevfik, he said:

"They say that you are operating the grocery shop ... And, in addition, fawning on Selim Pasha brings in a good deal of money ... The old man is rich, eh?"

"I talk a lot more often with Monsieur his son, my Lord."

"They write that your daughter also is Mistress's toady … She is said to have shaken her navel at her command … The two of you together earn a lot of money, is that not so?"

The cheekbones of Tevfik's sallow face flushed piece by piece as if he had cought typhoid again. He gulped, his hands resting on his knees shook.

"I do not take money from them, my Lord."

"Why?"

"They were said to be good to my girl when I was exiled … They brought her up, they educated her."

"Now let's skip the matter of your daughter. You, thank God that I am Interior Minister! For, if not?"

"What crime have I committed, my Lord?"

"They sent information to the Sultan through me. Fortunately, I did not let it pass further."

His voice was full of menace, he struck the papers on top of his desk:

"It is said that in your room Lord Hilmi and his friend assemble until midnight setting up conspiracies against the Sultan and organizing depravities . . . You should well know, my eyes and my ears are everywhere."

"It's all a lie, sir, they are not at all that kind of man. And as for me, the very instant it happened, I would tell them never to come to my house any more."

"Don't do that, don't say that ..."

Zati Bey's eyes looked at Tevfik with deep meaning:

"Let them come much more often than formerly, let them talk, be talkative in front of them, open their mouths, come to me and give me news of what they said. It would be better for you, Tevfik old fellow."

"If you are telling me to be a spy, this work I cannot do, my Lord."

"Our old clown's nose is certainly in the air!"

"God forbid, my Lord, I, I cannot do such things."

If it turns the stomach of some men when they are offered frogs, or snails, or pigs to eat -- even in the biggest restaurants and on golden serving dishes -- there are also men who are nauseated when they are ask to spy. Tevfik was one of them. So great was the aversion he felt, so much did this aversion increase together with an expression of weakness, debility, and sickness, that he suddenly began to wail like a child.

"Very well, very well . . . Let me close this matter now. Only let me go to the main point. You are said to be putting on Karagöz, to be doing public story-telling!"

Tevfik's tears dried up. At last the blow that he had expected and truly feared had fallen on his brain. Whatever happened, he wanted to hide the confusion of the guilty from Zati Bey. He said to himself "Why did I embark upon this business, why did I imitate this fellow? I thought I did it in secret but certainly his spies figured it out," but his eyes dully and stupidly, without meaning or intelligence were looking at Zati Bey and his lips were saying: "If you command me, I'll give it all up, my Lord."

"Don't give it up but pay attention. Remember how much it cost Mr. Nef to make fun of great men."

"I do not know Mr. Nef, my Lord."

"It is natural that you don't know him. He is from quite a long time ago. He too wanted to satirize ministers, and the Sublime Porte strangled him, threw his body into the sea. He does not even have a grave on the face of the world. And moreover he was not a low public story-teller like you, but a great poet. However, don't be nervous. In this century that type of thing doesn't happen anymore. But know that if I want I can exile you to Gehenna. But you are the head of a household. I am sorry for you. It is clearly known that we are men with hearts …"

Tevfik looked at his hands. He clenched his teeth and didn't say anything. Zati Bey came over and clapped him on the shoulders with a sauciness that reminded him of the old days.

"While it is in my mind, let me ask, why have you not brought your daughter to kiss my wife's skirt, ungrateful rascal?"

With a somewhat cracked voice, Tevfik responded without lifting his eyes: "Her upbringing is not suitable to bring into the presence of Mistress."

"Did she not then receive education in Pasha's mansion?"

His daughter … his daughter … oh if only he could have made this loathsome rascal forget he had a daughter … Now again he was looking at Zati Bey with an innocent expression:

"That is correct, my Lord. But nevertheless my girl is the grand-daughter of a neighborhood

Imam … She is the sneeze from his nose[39], indeed a well-known hafiz, my Lord."

"They told me that she sings beautiful songs …"

Zati Bey was a little indecisive. Could there have been talk in the journal about songs?

"Where would that be, my Lord? She only reads ashir, the ilahi … She goes for the response. If there is some Mevlit …"

With his hand Zati Bey cut short Tevfik's chatter. His curiosity concerning Rabia was gone with the same speed that it had come.

"I will tell Mistress. This type of things squeezes my insides into an evil condition. Just so you know, listen to me, I am not a man to bargain with."

He looked at his watch, started up.

"I am going to the Palace. As for you, I will tell you one more thing for your own good: don't put on Karagöz, do public story-telling, and such like … You will know if I have any more complaints."

Tevfik stood up. He kissed the skirt of his black jacket, saluted him. This time his escape was cheap.

Zati Bey clapped his hands, and the pop eyed spy came into the room.

"Take Mr. Tevfik to his house in the carriage. Take these five lira and give them to his daughter. The child may have been frightened. Well Tevfik, you can thank God. If you have any problem, come to me."

---

[39] In English the spitting image.

His shoulders forward, his hands at his side, when he left the room he really believed that he was a noble, generous man.

Chapter Twenty-one

His face alone was like a Jesus imagined by one of the fourteenth century painters. He had the expression of someone who has come down to earth from Heaven to create brotherhood and well-being among men. Although his body belonged to Abdulhamid's palace, his spirit dwelt in the sixteenth century. He was the second chamberlain[40].

In the palace environs, they knew him as a man who did his duty with the tidiness of a machine. There he had not one friend, not even an acquaintance. In his personal life, even this man who said very little and was official, was more official, more voiceless. But his personality, like a light perceived behind thick curtains, made itself felt on the outside.

In his house, he collected antique daggers, book bindings, and old English clocks. And besides this he grew rare roses in the garden of his waterside mansion, and sometimes carved sandal wood back scratchers. These two hobbies of his brought him closest to Selim Pasha of all the strangers who came and went at the Palace.

But all these tasks were things that remained outside of his whole life. In some deep place of the emotionless air of his spirit occupying his spare time with the scientific world of the sixteenth century, there was a totally unexpected corner, a little indefinite and a little mystical. And in that corner dwelt a desire to write a verse after a pattern found in the Dervish writer Rumi.

Because of this, he was very devoted to Vehbi Dede … Because of this, besides his library in French, he had a rich collection of the works of old Turkish, Persian and Arab poets. But in the richest library of Istanbul, there was not one single book relating to his own time.

---

[40] Ikinci (=second) mabeyinci, from the "mabeyn" door (porte), separating selamlik from harem. The chamberlain had an important role in the Sublime Porte as designate of the Sultan.

That the second chamberlain was this type of man, and at the same time controlled the security and favor of the Sultan, was not so difficult to explain as it appeared. He considered the order of society just as unchangeable and absolute as the order of nature. The Sultan, in his opinion, was a representative of the social and political order. The Sultan was a well-bred man. His voice never rose, his behavior was never harsh to anyone, he ordered even the darkest of his crimes with a smiling and refined attitude. Without counting the most unpardonable of his crimes a lack of refinement, the second chamberlain turned a blind eye to this ugly painful side of his master. The jealous intrigues of rival power bases, their thefts passing all boundaries, the scandals of privileges bought and sold openly, turning the country into a peeled onion, bribes, bargains ... He looked at all of these like storms determined by the seasons. Just as when lightning struck and the heavens rumbled he drew the curtains and stuffed his thin fingers into his ears, when these moral whirlwinds and disasters blew outside, there was a thick curtain over his brain and two moral fingers stuffing up his ears.

Basically the second chamberlain was not directly concerned in the ugly side of the Palace. The Sultan, because he enjoyed the conversation of elegant men, for the most part debated with him and generally commissioned him to perform honors, favors, benevolences, and the Sultan's ceremonial entry. The second chamberlain was not compelled to consider what sort of vileness or boorishness these prizes were recompensing. And besides, at no time whatsoever did he want to straighten up or change the world, nor did he believe it was needed. Change in his opinion was untidiness, frank anarchy. Because of this, the position of this man who had not tasted the appetite for either fame or esteem or reputation or glory was the most secure of anyone in the fickle air of the Palace. The Sultan felt himself secure and safe from any conspiracy by the side of a man so devoid of ambition.

That day something communicated by a civil servant had seriously disquieted his heart. This time he was about to relay not a compliment but a scolding both to Selim Pasha, whom he welcomed to his presence, and to Zati Bey, whom he did not. Standing at the head of his table, with penetrating small eyes whose color was hard to determine in their narrow slits, his thin fingers were toying with a pencil sharpener. He was not paying any attention to the man in the armchair, who talked as he waved his arms and legs and made as much racket as a street vendor.

Selim Pasha came in with his shoulders a little sunken, his brows sulky. He gave a cold greeting to the man in the armchair. The second chamberlain, after pointing him to the armchair by the side of the table, began to talk without sitting:

"Evidence has lately come to the Sultan that pamphlets and newspapers sowing confusion and disorder have entered into the nation with greater frequency than usual."

Selim Pasha stared at Zati Bey with meaningful and contemptuous eyes. And in profiting from the secret question in the second chamberlain's voice, he immediately said:

"They enter by means of foreign postal services. Our brother the Interior Minister being young and knowledgeable about the necessities of our era, is occupied (he tugged on his beard) with foreign institutions. My age, my old head, compels me to treat the enemies of the Sultan -- even if they be foreign -- too harshly. Especially if the sultan's security is in question, I would not recoil from dragging an ambassador to the bastinado. Whereas the weakness of our brother for foreigners, especially Young Turks -- God forbid -- his courtesy is well known throughout the world."

Zati Bey said: "Would you turn up your nose at those who are called 'Young Turks', if it was your son? Lately all types of naughty pamphlets have been coming under the name of Monsieur your son."

"Give me the proof, please."

"Unfortunately, I cannot. The papers that come for His Lordship your Son's name pass by foreign postal services. It is not lawful for us to have envelopes of foreigners searched. There is a bitter truth and obstacle called Capitulation."

Selim Pasha looked for the second chamberlain's eyes. The latter said with utmost delicacy: "The Sultan does not suspect your loyalty. Perhaps His Lordship your Son is not aware of the harmful pamphlets coming in his name. According to the depositions of His Lordship the Minister, it was a foreigner, one of the civil servants of the French mails, who has provided this information. You will interrogate once His Lordship your Son."

"Please forgive me, my Lord. If my son has joined with the enemies of the Royal Personage, he will endeavor most of all to keep this from me. If I tell him what I know, he will not stop with a denial, but will tell his accomplice, perhaps his accomplices. The most basic police rule of a criminal investigation in this beginning phase of the inquiry, is for him not to know what I know."

Selim Pasha became silent.

His devotion to the sultan -- like Zati Bey's -- did not rest on material advantages. For him there was the concept of a "nation" that he was connected to with an almost "mystical" emotion. He was not capable of separating this notion of "nation" from that of the sultan.

"Whoever betrays the nation, I will give his soles such a bastinado that he will be an utter mess like pieces of cotton wool. Not only my very son, but even if he were a princeling, the apple of the Royal Personage's eye, if he were a traitor I would not balk at sending him to Fizan on foot."

After these words, which he spoke shooting fire from his eyes, he took a more respectful pose. He turned to the second chamberlain:

"Please make this my petition known to the Sultan: I am convinced that the Lord Minister has conscientiously carried out his duties in this matter. As soon as my son and his friends had become objects of suspicion, it was necessary to put them under observation and if perchance they entered the French post office, as soon as they left to have the envelopes searched."

Zati Bey leaped up to defend himself. But the second chamberlain was walking straight to the door of the room. He closed the door behind himself and left. He was thinking how unseemly, how contrary to good breeding it was to talk of "soles attacked like pieces of cotton wool with the bastinado".

He returned twenty minutes later. In the center of the room, standing up, he gave notice of yet another command:

"His majesty sends greetings to the two of you. At the present time, they have commanded their slave Selim Pasha to discharge the office of investigating the question of the importation of injurious papers. They did not feel that Zati Bey had sufficient experience to disentangle this delicate question. Unfortunately, among students, especially military students, there is an injurious excitement. You, Your Excellency Pasha, will investigate the question, you will take the measures that seem necessary, and you will give the Sultan daily reports. If, as I think, you two are occupied, I will not detain you further.

He walked to the door and opened it. Zati Bey went in front. Again a red satin purse found the palm of Pasha's hand. The second chamberlain bent over his ear, and whispered: "a token of the Sultan's appreciation."

This was the first gratuity-purse that burned Pasha's fingers. It was even as if a flame passed straight from his finger-tips and took hold of his heart. His devotion to the nation and the sultan had dropped him into a bitter situation, being forced to investigate his son. He accepted that. But to take money for this! How right was the poet who said: "Being near to a ruler is a stinging flame."

Chapter Twenty-two

"The person or persons who stood accused of introducing harmful documents into the land that his Excellency the Sultan had entrusted to their stewardship began to be under surveillance. On the information of his Lordship the Interior Minister, every single person who had been found in relations with the Son of Your Servant was put under surveillance. Meanwhile, when the piano teacher Peregrini, who frequented the French post office, left the post office, a hand package with what appeared to be newspapers on top was seemingly stolen by pick-pockets. An hour was stolen, to fashion event on top of event, as if it was normal modern police action. When the package had been found upon his complaint, a little afterwards it was returned. The letters were from a French musician; the package was an Italian book. It was discovered to be a pamphlet about Hell written by a rascal named Dante. The letters and the book were presented. A petition should be presented about the laws of capitulation and when not to put off to another day the question of throwing out foreign agents and institutions, respectfully submitted . . ."

This was Selim Pasha's first report. The second began thus:

"Hilmi has asked your servant for permission to take his wife, who is suffering from asthma, to Beirut for a change of air. This permission was granted. Two civil servants have settled on his trail. His arrest has been ordered as soon as they judge that he might attempt to flee. In Beirut they will investigate with whom he comes in contact, his correspondence will be subjected to a close inspection. The scoundrels will have been taken into custody in five or ten days, respectfully submitted ..."

It was so evident that Pasha had regained his old credit with the Sultan that Miss Sabiha understood this as well. But in spite of this his face was still anxious, abstracted. His behavior was especially strange with his wife. When he came face to face with Miss Sabiha, he would turn his head, would recoil from looking into her eyes.

This situation obtained until the first coded telegram was received from Beirut and opened shortly thereafter. For the first days, Hilmi had not made contact with anyone. Nevertheless, if the guilt of his son became evident, he would punish him with every punishment -- and more -- he meted out to the Young Turks. At the same time, if his son were cleared of this crime, he would sacrifice to Eyup Sultan[41].

These two possibilities became stronger as days passed and Pasha became more hopeful, more sanguine. That evening he even revived one of his habits that he had long ago abandoned. He went to his wife's room to drink coffee and the nargile[42]. He would joke with Rabia and she would sing one or two compositions.

The girl had not yet arrived. After Mistress had decided to send a man, she came but she was anxious. "I was waiting for Tevfik, Mistress. He has not yet returned. I am worried."

"Where did he go?"

Rabia laughed. "He is like a child. To an old playing friend of his in Kadiköy. His mind and his thought are all playing."

"How playing?"

"He rummaged through an old trunk of his in the attic, took out a woman's costume, put it on, he went out very mincingly. His friend he said had just got married, he was going to make his wife jealous ... After his illness saying he was worn out he had shaved his moustache. If you saw him, even you would suppose he was a woman."

---

[41] Eyup Sultan, the standard bearer of the prophet and the last survivor of his inner circle, believed to have died in the siege of Istanbul in 668-669 and whose tomb is in the Eyup Sultan mosque in Istanbul, constructed by Mehmet the conqueror after Costantinople finally fell to the Ottoman Turks.

[42] In Turkish, one "drinks" the nargile, rather than "smoking" it.

Pasha said: "Even your father, if I catch him wearing woman's clothes, I will bastinado him."

"In these times one does not beat people up. In Mr. Hilmi's good-bye dinner they were drinking the frothy beverage, they entered upon every merriment, every one was serenading him. Zati Bey, after shouting and chastising them, did not let out a peep."

The bailiff's wife opened the door and said: "Mr. Rana the assistant wants to see Pasha in the selamlik."

An event that had just taken place had impelled Mr. Rana to come to the mansion at this hour. It certainly had to be important. Selim Pasha went to the selamlik in his evening clothes.

The assistant was a man with a long nose like a bird's beak, and a crooked chin. His sunken eyes had no lashes and this nudity made him look like a reptile. The fact that his chin was so small and warped was not, as was generally thought, in Mr. Rana a sign of irresolution. On the contrary, both in appearance and disposition he resembled a bird of prey.

Pasha asked with a smile:

"What's up, Rana Bey? Don't tell me you've come at this hour to inform me that you've arrested a man in woman's clothing!"

"How did you know?"

Pasha took a breath. They must have caught Tevfik in woman's clothing, and with the police mind-set have given a secret meaning to it. He asked more cheerfully:

"Is the girl not Tevfik?"

"Himself, but from where did you learn this?"

"He is a grocer in a small street. I have known him from childhood. In the Zuhuri orta oyunu he took on the female role. His weakness is to put on women's clothing. Now I'm attached to his daughter. The girl grew up under my care, I educated her . . . The rascal gives me another cause for worry. He imitates the Interior Minister . . ."

This last worry was so much to Pasha's taste that he laughed. His assistant did not laugh.

"The matter is much more serious, Pasha. We arrested the rascal in woman's clothing coming out of the French Post Office. On him was a big package of harmful informations."

Selim Pasha felt a faintness as if a fist had pounded his belly. The hope awoken by the coded dispatches received from Beirut began to fade. In his mind he had formed every event into a shape that was not very far from reality. Hilmi had invited this wretch, they had drunk what they called the "frothy thing", or Champagne. Afterwards, having said whatever was said, he had persuaded him to smuggle the harmful informations. Oh the contemptible boy... Stooping to hide behind this clown, cowardly, despicable man! Selim Pasha could recall no greater blow to his honor. Hilmi could be found a traitor ... be exiled ... even be executed. All of these things were capable of tearing apart a father's heart. But to know his son was coward-ly, contemptible . . . There was no father in this world carrying a pain like this one.

Rana Bey did not perceive the effect of these bitternesses of the heart on Pasha's face. On the contrary, he became the stern and vigilant Justice Minister of his working hours.

"Sit, Rana Bey. Tell me the story from the beginning."

"As you know, our men were stationed at the entrance of the French Post Office. You know one was a chestnut-seller. Here dolled-up women continuously came and went. But the detectives, on your orders, left them alone. This time a tall woman dressed in a yeldirme and an old-fashioned dress came. That a woman dressed in this fashion would go into the foreign post office exited the detective's suspicion. But they did nothing, saying that perhaps she was the nanny of one of the little ladies. When the woman came out, she paused in front of the chestnut-seller and bought chestnuts. The hair on her hands attracted attention. Then when she lifted her skirt to take out money, a man's shoe was seen on her feet. At once they leaped on her trail. In a lonely side street, on pretext of bothering her, they pulled off her head-covering, and together with the veil false hair was left in their hands. This evening they brought her straight to the gendarmes. I have looked at the documents, they are important."

"Do they have an address?"

"It appears that the rascal tore off the address in the post office. We have not got him to confess. And our torturer Muzaffer we even got to work on him. It's very unusual for a female impersonator to show such fortitude. But we have not come to the end."

Pasha stood up and said:

"Wait for me one or two minutes while I get dressed."

Chapter Twenty-three

All the lamps of the prefecture were lit, among all the detectives there was the joy and pride of hunters who have captured a rare prey . . . two enormous assistants brought their prey into Selim Pasha's presence.

Tevfik's clothes were disheveled, but still preserved the remnants of his feminine attire. On his face, white lead, rouge and kohl running together made two parallel black, red and white tracks stretching from his eyes to his chin -- tracing his tears -- while around his eyes, his nose and cheeks were covered with black and purple bruises, inside which his ever soft, chestnut-colored eyes, dull and bewildered, seemed for the first time in his life to have forgotten how to laugh. The lower part of the black yeldirme he was wearing hung in pieces, muddy everywhere, and on his shoulders he saw a few blood stains. Did he recognize him? Did he understand? Was it possible for him to comprehend these things?

In this condition, disrupting Tevfik both inside and out, taking away his intelligence, Selim Pasha recognized the hand of the torturer. This last, his hand on Tevfik's shoulders, with the complaisance and willingness of the hunting dog waiting on the orders of his master, was gazing into Selim Pasha's eyes. This obese man, although charged with putting dangerous political suspects to the question, had nothing fearful in his appearance. He looked much more like an ex-wrestler who had given himself up to eating and drinking after retiring from the ring.

He had the many layered chin fluttering from the height of his tightly buttoned collar, the flabby cheeks and the fleshy brow of a man who does not reflect ... friendship reminiscent of an elephant in his small friendly sunken eyes. But his claws could crush the ear of the accused into dust, so that he became not only deaf, but blind. And these hands had caressed Tevfik's ear dust a few times.

"Give him a chair, give him a cigarette."

They sat Tevfik down in a chair, they put a cigarette into his hands. Rana Bey the assistant struck the match with his own hand, but Tevfik's fingers did not grasp the cigarette, his hands remained on his knees.

Muzaffer was ready for duty. "Is the rascal anything but a liar?"

Pasha silenced him with a harsh voice: "You get out, and leave the rascal to himself."

When they were alone, Pasha bent down and looked closely into Tevfik's face. And Pasha's memory, for the first time in the conduct of his duty, played a trick on him. Tevfik reminded him of an old horse that he had known from infancy and had loved more than his father or his mother. One day the animal broke its foot and his manservant had said that there was nothing else to do but put a bullet in the horse's head. Now Tevfik's eyes were looking at him with the expression of the wounded horse waiting for help from him. At last, his hand barely grazed the shoulder that had spattered blood over the black yeldirme.

"Tell me everything. Who sent you to the French post office, dressed this way? I will punish him, even if it was my son himself… We are men here whom the Sultan has charged with justice…"

Now a life-giving current coursed through the face that a moment before was suffused with the dimness of death. Perhaps he understood what Pasha had said. But in truth, in the deepest layer of his consciousness, an image had been woken up. In that place was a Tevfik, chatting and laughing with a frothy, sweet drink in his hand. A friendly, brotherly voice was bending down to his ear, and saying:

"Don't tell anyone I sent you to the post office; tear off the address inside the post office and throw it away."

Now that voice was repeating yet another time, the things that had been said. It was not what it said, but the very significance of the voice that made Tevfik tremble. It was a voice that relied on Tevfik's humanity, that entrusted its physical security and its reputation to his fidelity, his brotherliness, his courage. There were still a few more Tevfiks, a few more!

Tevfiks drinking the drink at the tables of great men, entertaining those around him, making them laugh . . . But each one was still a clown . . . a made-up face kicked in the teeth, that you had to spit into! A Tevfik that was no different from a bear or monkey entertaining the market-place crowd with a ring in its nose or a chain around its neck! The primordial artist of the East…Whereas this voice, this Tevfik at the table was a man…like every one.

He closed his eyes, his lips muttered.

Rana Bey and Pasha together as one bent down, and approached their ears to this muttering mouth.

"I will not say, I will not say, by God . . ."

Pasha's hands with their thin fingers like tiger claws again caressed his shoulders.

"Only tell me, Tevfik. Especially don't hide it from me if it was my son who sent you to the post office. Was it Hilmi? Tell me … I give you my oath I will not have you beaten any longer … And your punishment, if you confess, will be lighter. I will exile you to a near-by place, I will settle you with a monthly stipend. I will send Rabia to be with you … Confess, was it Hilmi?"

Hardly had Rabia's name left his mouth when the shoulders under his hands trembled.

Pasha again bent down and looked into Tevfik's face. Tears were flowing over the black, white and red streaks extending from his eyes to his chin, his black and blue lips were fluttering. But not a single sound passed from his mouth.

"Rana Bey, this is enough for today. Tell them to wash his hands and face and put something on him suitable for a man. Don't let Muzaffer put him to the question without asking me."

"Should I have clothes brought from his house?"

"No, no, buy them in the street. I'll give you money. His girl must not learn of this!" They took Tevfik from Pasha's room, took him away. And Pasha at once sat down at the head of his table and read the documents that were found on the suspect.

Most of them were newspapers and pamphlets published in Switzerland or Paris. These, to Selim Pasha, seemed nonsensical, like utter craziness or ravings of an old woman. But it was not the journals and pamphlets that made him think. That was a hand-written letter, written to an unknown man. Supposedly, it was preparing a general rebellion to depose the Sultan. Supposedly, there were very many men who supported this. It even mentioned many well-known names. Perhaps this was a tissue of lies. How many times such things had happened. But in spite of this Pasha knew that he would make a large number of arrests. There would be a lot of interrogations that the torturer would be charged with . . . And perhaps, perhaps Hilmi would be among them.

Pasha put the informations to one side. He selected a pen on the table, examined its tip attentively and wrote his report to the Palace.

"Send this with a detective ... Tell them afterwards to bring me a washtub, a pitcher and a prayer rug. After namaz I will stretch out and take a nap in this armchair."

It was morning and Istanbul was waking up. As soon as Pasha had finished namaz, he stretched out in the armchair, tucked his head into his armpit, and his mind passed away.

The racket in the street increased. From afar was coming the sound of a barrel organ and a dream appeared to Pasha. It was a feast-day. Hilmi was six years old. He was wearing the uniform of a pasha . .. his trouser legs below the knees were untidy, on his shoulders were great huge epaulets ... A tin sword tied at his waist, he was swaggering about shaking his sleeves like a peacock cub. A young woman whose white hands were full of rings clapped her hands. Her hazel eyes glittered and burned.

The sounds of the barrel organ approached. The boy stood still, listened to the street, and then tried to tear the tin sword from his waist and throw it down, shouting at the top of his lungs:

"I want the barrel organ, I want the barrel organ ..."

Selim Pasha was sweating from anxiety. Why didn't they shut up this spoiled boy? Why did he himself not give two slaps to that cheeky mouth?

The sounds of the barrel organ were cut off. The sun lit up the Justice Minister's head. Drops of sweat dripped from his forehead onto his cheeks. He had an evil anxiety. Half asleep, half waking, he said to the child in his dream:

"This time I will give you your punishment ..."

Chapter Twenty-four

For four days Rabia did not hear from her father. One by one Rakim visited Tevfik's old friends who lived in Kadiköy. Had Tevfik come to them four days ago, dressed as a woman? Everyone shook his head and looked very strangely into the dwarf's face. Rakim explained that they had thought him missing for a little while. But the bitterest thing was waiting for him by the shop door to extinguish each evening the light of hope burning like the two flames of honey colored eyes.

Again Sinekli Bakkal was living a new life with Tevfik's adventure. Again there was a life drama. Every day, the neighbors called at the shop asking for news; in every house, in the street and at the fountain head they talked of Tevfik's disappearance. The neighborhood children played the game of "kidnapping Uncle Tevfik to the mountain."

If Rabia had not been so distracted, she would have found Miss Sabiha's manner very suspicious. This friendly woman, who had always been so interested in things relating to Tevfik, now appeared almost indifferent. When she confessed her trouble to her, when she begged her to have Pasha search for Tevfik like a bulldog, she would plant her eyes on the ceiling without responding. And for four days whenever Rabia ran to Pasha's room, she would find it shut tight as a clam.

Although Miss Sabiha had learned the next day of the disaster that had fallen on Rabia's head with Tevfik's arrest, Pasha's admonition to her not to tell Rabia was not so unnatural. But she was suspicious when he said: "After I discover his associates, I will tell her." Why when he said "associates" had Pasha's eyes suddenly avoided his wife's eyes?

And the woman immediately understood. This man, tied to a host of dry words like Sultan, nation and duty, suspected his own son. Ah, what would Miss Sabiha have done not to share this suspicion of Pasha! But now there was such a fear inside her that … Five times a day she prayed that Tevfik would die without giving up his accomplices ... However much she beseeched God with a deep ambition that his tongue be tied up, if Rabia found out, if she saw her father, she would persuade him perhaps to betray his confederates ... As for Tevfik...

After four days, this calamitous atmosphere of the mansion spread to the street, even enveloped all of Istanbul. A great number of arrests had commenced. This news was muttered from ear to ear, from ear to ear it was bruited about that Selim Pasha had become the most inauspicious, the most tyrannical face of Istanbul. My beloved Sultan couldn't want this, could he? All the men around him fanned his delusions. Who knows what tricks there were? His spies filled the earth and with what ranks, what decorations, what money they were filled up!

The people of Sinekli Bakkal crouched down in this atmosphere of terror like animals sensing the storm's approach. Sometimes they would crowd around the street corner and whisper about this matter, and every one's eye would dart about, and as soon as a footfall was heard, all would be silent . . . Even the women taking water at the fountain, when they heard the sound of Selim Pasha's carriage at the corner, would run away hugging the walls.

A few days after everyone except Rabia had come to the belief that Tevfik was among the prisoners, Miss Sabiha informed her of the danger that hung over her father's head:

"Pasha is convinced he is innocent . . . He will be exiled if he doesn't explain what the business he did was. Don't worry, Rabia. Pasha will release him. I don't know what evidence they have shown, but you go to the Prefecture tomorrow morning and bring tobacco and underwear.

And early the next morning, a bundle on her shoulder, she appeared at the door of the Prefecture. Rakim had wrapped himself tightly around the hem of her yeldirme. In the neighborhood coffee-house, he had heard of the tortures inflicted on the suspects, he had even heard an exaggerated tale of the head torturer. He had not discussed any of these things with

Rabia. But his knees and his heart had collapsed like two empty inner-tubes, and his jaw was frozen. In spite of this, with his turban ajar, his eyes jumping out of their sockets and his shoes torn up, he stumbled along after Rabia.

Inside the corridors of the prefecture, with her package in her hand, fear in her eyes, and her voice hoarse she appeared to be the ghost of a woman. No one took notice of this young girl, with the height of a cypress and the eyes of a child, or the wretched dwarf clinging to her skirt.

Functionaries went in and out of the rooms with papers or trays of coffee in their hands, but no one stopped and asked Rabia what she wanted.

A fat man with a laughing face approached Rabia: "Who are you looking for, sister?"

"God bless you, my brother. I want to see the female impersonator, Tevfik."

The hugely obese man scratched his head and his elephant-like eyes sank completely into the fleshy folds of his cheeks. "No one is allowed to see him. If you want, leave your package, I'll give it to him."

"But I am his daughter."

"Unless you have brought a written order from Pasha, even his daughter or his mother cannot be let in to see him."

"If the Lord Pasha were here, he would give me permission."

The girl's voice was full of hope. The fat man again scratched his head, again he puckered up his eyes. "Let me go and see if I can find an assistant detective."

He plunged into the room which they were standing in front of. After a minute that seemed long to the girl, he came out, opened the door, and took the girl inside, motioning to a place behind the door where the dwarf could wait.

Rana Bey, after thinking it over, had only admitted Rabia to his presence because he knew she was connected to the mansion. But his he had firmly decided to get rid of her fast.

"You cannot see your father today, my daughter. When you are permitted, I will let you know."

Her back inside the loose-fitting yeldirme seemed to become straighter, and her thin chin rose up.

"I absolutely must see him today."

"Impossible . . . Look, Pasha is coming, tell him about it . . . If he gives you permission, I'll let you in."

Rabia did not notice that the Justice Minister was a far different man from the old Selim Pasha she had come to know in the mansion, who was courteous, even kindly. The green sparks in her honey-colored eyes were kindled with hope. She confessed her trouble to him with an absolute confidence:

"They will not let me see my father, Lord Pasha."

Inside the black yeldirme, the wretched meager body billowed, inside of which she begged for help, looking at Selim Pasha with such trusting, loving, beautiful eyes! These things did not alter Pasha's Justice Minister mask, but dried out his throat a little. He coughed:

"Today it is impossible, Rabia. Leave the package, go home. In a few days ... don't ... don't ... don't cry ...!

Pasha's voice was not harsh at all. But it was so resolute that the fire in the girl's eyes at once died down. She couldn't see around her from her eyes because of her tears falling like water. All of a sudden her feet were cut off underneath her, a mist enveloped her eyes. With sobs tearing at her throat she collapsed around Pasha's feet, and wrapped her scrawny arms around Pasha's knees like a drowning man embracing a life raft.

"I won't go home, Lord Pasha ... Only let me see his face from the open door . . . if he is only alive ... only that much. Have you ... you have not killed my father?"

God help us! How would Selim Pasha save himself from this difficult, this ridiculous situation? Through the open door, his eyes fell upon Rakim's face. He made a hand signal. Like a rubber ball, the dwarf bounded into the middle of the room, caught hold of the girl's shoulders, and tried at once both to pull and push the girl, saying continuously:

"Don't make Pasha angry, Rabia, you'll come back . . . Come on, my chick!"

A wretched voice trying to console a wretched child! A crooked voice of a dwarf! Rabia never ever forgot it. Because in that big room, what was inside the broad chests of men lined up standing tall was in Rabia's opinion nothing. Among them Rakim was like a mole, but alone in his chest beat the heart of a man!

Rabia stood up, her hand in the dwarf's hand, her shoulders drooping, and left the room. Pasha called out after the dwarf:

"Don't let me see you in this street if you don't want trouble!"

In the corridor, it wasn't the dwarf dragging her, she was pulling the dwarf. The prefecture made her feel like a nightmare, she wanted to escape as soon as possible from the dream.

She had almost forgotten the cause of the pain that burned her heart. In front of the door, some one said from behind: "Leave the package, sister. Tevfik doubled up called for tobacco; an hour earlier I emptied my cigarette box in front of him."

The girl turned around with lightning speed and extended the package. Of the men who were all tools of tyranny, this hell-hound, this huge man seemed like the one man in the eye of the needle. Rabia's honey colored eyes looked at him in gratitude:

"See that my father is well, my brother!"

It was natural to look at him that way. The head torturer Muzaffer, outside of his fixed duty to make suspects confess crimes, what is truth and what is false, when orders came from above, was a man who tried to please everyone.

Rabia didn't look around until she passed the corner of the prefecture. Only when she had turned into the street on the other side did her knees give out, and she collapsed on the marble stoop of a house door. She began to cry with a violent shaking of her shoulders. The passersby --the dwarf was loitering by her side -- took her for a beggar. One handed her money.

After this, without stopping, without interruption, she returned with Rakim to the house. She did not cry any more. She crouched down on a cushion, without talking. Like an animal experiencing an unendurable pain of unknown cause, she whimpered there . . .

Chapter Twenty-five

"What is it, Bilal? Is someone sick at home? My mother isn't sick, is she?"

As Bilal opened that carriage door at the quay, Hilmi's eyes riddled his face with holes, trying to comprehend the meaning of his closed and darkened expression.

He had just arrived from Beyrut, had just disembarked from the steamboat. He was so shocked at the change in his future brother-in-law's expression that he did not even ask who were the two civil servants standing behind Bilal.

"It's nothing, truly it's nothing. You wait in the carriage; I will send the baggage with Shevket Aya, I'll be back."

As Hilmi, his eyes on back of the carriage driver, opened the carriage door, deep in thought, Shevki jumped on his breast and wrapped his arms in Hilmi's; they sat down and without pausing to think of the two men waiting ten paces distant from the carriage but in a low voice he began to recount what had befallen Tevfik. Without preamble and without going through all the details, he discussed that letter that had worried Selim Pasha and the whole Palace.

"The head torturner Muzaffer has put Tevfik to the question, but up 'til now he has not betrayed us. For goodness' sake, keep your mouth shut and do not make anything clear by your expression . . . "

Before Hilmi found time to answer, Bilal came back and sat down opposite them. The three did not speak a single word until the carriage drew near to Aksaray. Hilmi, as if he couldn't digest the situation's peculiar type of ugliness, started to say to himself: "Honor, honor ..."

But Shevki's hand, with the nimbleness of a tiger, covered his mouth and he was almost swearing at Hilmi from between his teeth: "When great purposes are discussed, the honor of an individual is dry vanity."

All of these things had made more of an impression on Bilal than on Hilmi. Bilal's white-eyelashed blue eyes quickly studied Shevki's swarthy face, savage with fanaticism. His head, having grown up in Macedonia province, was accustomed to thinking that every trick was legal in order to win in war. Perhaps they had taught him something strange called Tanzimat[43] literature in the Galatasaray High School . . . Now Shevki, that Istanbulite who had graduated first in his class, had spoken with a refinement that Bilal's uncle would have called bookish. His lips reddened, and learned by heart everything about Shevki.

When the carriage stopped at the mansion door, Hilmi did not detain his friend. He climbed the staircase virtually two stairs at a time to see his mother as fast as possible.
But when he entered his mother's room, he found her expression as strange as Shevki's.

Miss Sabiha asked neither how Dürnev's journey was, nor Hilmi's. Her eyes widened from fear, from excitement her voice stuttered and stammered. She could hardly tear her eyes away from the door, as if someone would come and grab Hilmi and carry him off.

"Have you heard what has befallen Tevfik? God be praised, boy, he has not betrayed anyone. Someone must have tipped those men off, if they paid attention, so that they would not betray themselves ... or even, even so that they might slip off!

"Do you know for sure who they were, mother?

"No, no, and I don't want to know. I pray for their safety day and night. And if Tevfik informs on them, he himself will not even escape punishment ... A few more women will cry

---

[43] The tanzimat was a modernization of the Ottoman Empire toward the end of the 19th century. "The reforms attempted to integrate non-Muslims and non-Turks more thoroughly into Ottoman society by enhancing their civil liberties and granting them equality throughout the Empire." From Wikipedia.

. . . A whole company of hearths will be extinguished!"

With a sudden catch in her throat, she wrapped her arms around Hilmi and squeezed him as if she were going to drown, sobs that she wanted to imprison in her withered chest pressed against Hilmi's chest tearing at her throat. Tears ran down her neck from Hilmi's collar and she was entreating Hilmi, talking as if she wanted to prohibit him from at once turning over and seizing Tevfik's supposed confederates:

"Don't do it, my child, I will be your dog, don't do it, spare your old mother!"

Hilmi unfastened his mother's arms from his neck, withdrew a little, and looked into his old mother's face. Her eyes were swollen from crying, her miserable face had suddenly grown ten years older.

Her powdered, rouged mask that had not yet collapsed beyond repair, reminded him of an ancient whitewashed building. But the pain and fear in her hazel eyes that were still young and spirited were unraveling Hilmi's heart. And he did not recognize until these moments that he loved his mother with a deep compassion.

To this mother who asked him to sacrifice his honor for his personal salvation, he was so devoted, so devoted that …

"Pasha desires you, Hilmi Bey."

The sudden entrance of Miss Shükriye into the room brought him back to himself. He was going to go to his room to wash his hands and face and change, and then go and see his father. But when he left his mother's room, he was so exhausted that he said to himself:

"What is the sense in pulling a whole group of people into further calamity? And for a childish whim that does not really have a foundation. How could this regime be demolished with a piece of paper? I sent Tevfik to the post office, but certainly I cannot save him from punishment ... As Shevki has said, does bravery here not consist of empty boasting?" Moreover, one side of his nature was soft and easily captivated by foreign influences. But a power that he had not even known he possessed was hidden in him. And the voice of that power shouted:

"I wonder if you shrink from betraying yourself not from pity towards your mother, or from being involved in a purpose, but from pure cowardice?"

While he had withdrawn into his room, the thoughts chasing one another around his head were like a herd of crazy men knocking against each other and losing their identities and boundaries.

He washed his face. He brushed off his clothing. He sat down and tried to collect himself a little. In his heart, more than ever he felt a revolt and anger against harshness, against everything that forced tyrannized and anguished him. Even now these things unbecoming to his native country -- even if he used them to give a sacrificial laving to a tyrant -- were things that caused mischief and hatred. The world appeared to him to be an unbecoming wrestling arena. Those who revolted, who raised a rebellion against the Sultan and the government, all, all of them were men kneaded and formed from the same unbecoming dough. Only as individuals were they innocent, only as individuals were they wretched and sometimes even good.

How had it happened in the past when Hilmi had believed that everything happened according to human justice in the West? How had tyranny and despotism aflicted and made violence against the lives of those French revolutionaries with whom he had drunk sherbet in brightly lit rooms scented with jasmine from the windows?

He stood up. He carefully arranged his neck-tie in the mirror, and walked to his father's room.

On the way, he was saying to himself:

"For an individual, there is only one road to salvation, and that is, with Vehbi Dede, to consider the universe a dream of God which comes and passes."

Selim Pasha asked his son after his daughter-in-law's health, he asked how the trip was, he pointed to a place and sat him down. He himself did not sit down. He was calm and polite, but his expression was more official than ever. After quite a while, he also began to recount what had happened concerning Tevfik. In any event, Tevfik's probable accomplices awoke in him more pity than wrath. To such an extent that little by little his peace and quiet had begun to be destroyed.

"If I am able to catch the cowardly rascal who hides behind a clown . . ."

Hilmi's eyes saw Pasha's thin fingers had twisted around one another as if he was compressing the throat of an imaginary criminal. A bitter smile on his lips, he asked:

"Was there then more than one member of the group?"

"All of those bastards who are exposed, they will see the punishment of their crimes."

"Why are they bastards? Why is it a crime, to rebel against the Sultan's tyranny?"

"I don't understand."

"For instance, those whom you have reckoned guilty may also reckon you guilty."

"What did you say? What did you say?"

"Let us entertain this thought for a minute."

"Never. Not even for a moment. In the world, there is only one straight path, and only one crooked. The things that I believe are straight, what they believe is vain and useless. Do you understand? And do you not understand that you are acting contemptibly by hiding behind that clown?"

" . . ."

"Answer me!"

"I will not. Believe what you will, do whatever comes from your hands . . . understood?" A Hilmi holding his head up ... Almost forgetting to lisp, a tough and an open man!

"If I believed, you would now be beside Tevfik, Hilmi Bey. But you have not shown the courage of that rascal who wears women's clothing. If you had undergone what he has undergone . . . If you had once felt Muzaffer's paw on your ear wax, you would have betrayed your mother and your father, you would have begged for mercy as you kissed his hand and foot . . . you have the heart of a rabbit, you are cowardly and soulless!"

The bonds between a father and son were broken, separated, the myths of respect and education had been dispersed like fog. The two became enemies who wanted to leap on one another's throats and destroy each other. The elder's hands remained at his side, because he did not think his opponent worthy, even to raise his hand, or even to be beaten. The fists of the younger were in the air . . .

"Hilmi, go to your room. I will talk with your father, alone."

For two minutes, the two of them had not seen the woman standing, leaning on her cane by the door. The two came to and recovered something of their composure.

In the woman's voice, no trace remained of the weakness she had shown a half hour before, when she begged on Hilmi's behalf.

Hilmi was still enraged at his father -- to the point of still wanting to go and snap his throat with his fingers. But he yielded to his mother and went out.

188

Chapter Twenty-six

The second chamberlain opened the conversation.

"So Tevfik has not yet said who sent him to the Post Office. But perhaps he went on his own account."

Selim Pasha shook his head.

"Our diagnosis would not read that way. To attain to something intellectual, a Karagöz actor, an ignorant neighborhood grocer. No, no . . . He has others behind him."

"Zati Bey said that he imitated great men when he put on his shadow play and made refined allusions to disguise his thought. Does this not show him to be very crafty? Perhaps he is only a tricky and deceitful anarchist."

"Zati Bey is taken in by surface details if anyone makes an allusion satirizing traditions . . . He sets out to exile the satirist. For six hundred years, these imitations and allusions have taken place in the shadow play."

For a time, the two were quiet, thinking to themselves as they watched their cigarette smoke. Then Selim Pasha brought up the philosophical question he had frequently pondered of late:

"The rascal's heart is like a woman . . . so too is his head. The state, the government, politics, the Sultan ... He does not understand any of these things. I took him as my opponent, I talked to him. I tried to get it into his head that he does not have the importance of an ant. The individual is a grain of wheat, the state and the government is a grist-mill ... They crush each grain, and put into into the shape they want. We will make them forget this philosophy that prefers to start imitating the West, that presumes to appropriate decadent ideas for us. Rely on my word, my Lord. I believe that if one day the Young Turks come into the government, also they, as much as we do, or even more than we do, they will crush the individual!"

Pasha wiped off his sweat. His eyes were fixed in the distance. He seemed to be staring at the image of the machinery of an outmoded state, condemned to collapse along with himself. But a minute later, he went at the same subject from a different angle:

"Women … It is not fortunate when women meddle in government affairs. Because none of them understand this philosophy. But it is not because of lack of intelligence! Women have come and gone who managed the government like a performance behind the scenes. In everyone there is something that loses out to his emotions, like our Tevfik. For instance, if Tevfik had been a common clown, he would have confessed much more readily. If he had been a powerful man, he would not have cried. But the two things did not take place. He endured the blows of the torturer, he cried, he passed out, but he still did not betray the man whom he loved. Women are also like that. For example, take my wife … Suppose she had become grand vizier … Trust me, she would have administered the state with greater ability than the present grand vizier. But if any of her duties came into conflict with maternal feeling, not just the state that she managed, but all the states of the universe she would personally pull down."

An inner smile reminiscent of Vehbi Dede appeared on the second chamberlain's lips.

"The morals of love! Perhaps in some unknown future it will become the lawgiver . . . God willing."

He paused. The old man wanted to reveal the worm that gnawed at his heart. With a friendly and casual air, he said:

"Why are you so determined to believe that your son is guilty?"

Lately Pasha's dry face that resembled an eagle's skeleton had taken on an almost green color from worry and sleeplessness. But the second chamberlain's last words aroused two red fever spots in his cheek-bones.

"When he was in Beyrut, I too thought I believed in his innocence. Ah were I yet capable of believing! If you knew how we two souls have become enemies. When I found the opportunity, I explained that they had put Tevfik to the question. If he had the least speck of the conscience of a man, he would confess, I said. He clenched his teeth, his eyes were shifty, but instead of confessing he mocked me. Even at one point he was within an inch of raising his hand ... to me ... to his father! If you knew, from now on my house is a hell. My wife of forty years, that unsound lady has become incapable of looking into my face. She will die from her sorrow. Tevfik's girl, the child that I brought up as my own rightful child, does not set foot into the mansion. What have I done? I have become everybody's bogey-man. Should an old and faithful servant who is prepared to sacrifice his son for the sake of religion and the state receive this treatment?"

He narrowed his lip and paused. If he had continued, all his fortitude would have melted away. His face assumed the old stubborn, hard mask of the Justice Minister. He stood up. The second chamberlain also stood up.

"The time has come, Selim Pasha, to present to the Sultan what we think should be done with the prisoners. It is useless to make any further effort to get Tevfik to confess ..."

Pasha extended an envelope. Laconically, he said: "My petition."

On Wednesday, the second chamberlain communicated to Selim Pasha Sultan's will concerning the prisoners.

Bureaucrats of high and low grade, students whose number this time was very large, were exiled in utter confusion, half were sent to Tripoli, half to Yemen. It had not been clear to those, although their names were mentioned in the investigation and letter, that they had been made ready for the blow to fall. But if these had not been expelled from Istanbul, the Sultan's mind would have not been at peace. If the brow of this individual who was the foundation stone of the state, the single representative of religion and state, could find peace, a few, even a few hundred people would be sacrificed! Selim Pasha also was of this opinion.

Tevfik was exiled to Damascus. He would be left free in the city. Pasha was pleased. But it puzzled him, where this affection that separated him from the other exiles came from. The second chamberlain said:

"The Sultan has been pleased with the impartial position you adopted viz-a-viz your son. He has been thinking about a way of both putting your conscience at ease and breaking Hilmi Bey of his inappropriate fancy for mischievous literature."

Pasha said to himself:

"I wonder what this preamble goes with? What are they going to do to Hilmi?" But he was silent. The second chamberlain continued:

"The Sultan has appointed Hilmi Bey Assistant Governor of Damascus. Normally this is an honorary Assistantship. This time Hilmi Bey will be compelled to dwell in the city. Soon, to please you, the Sultan will pardon a fault in him that he has attributed to youthful indiscretions, and will find another appointment for him."

Selim Pasha's conscience was in fact somewhat relieved. The fault of the other exiles had not even been as apparent as that of Hilmi. But in spite of this his throat dried up and his hands became like ice. The second chamberlain kept on:

192

"All of these must embark early tomorrow. We will assign them the government boat the Lord of the Sea. Please take care of what is necessary. When the time comes for the Sultan to go out for the Friday Selamlik, the steam-boat must be outside of the Bosporus."

Selim Pasha was still silent.

"It's natural if you want to make preparations, to give the news to the families. No one will bring his family with him, but before the steam-boat sets sail the families can go to the boat. He has commanded you to take every preparation for the city to be at peace."

Pasha gave an official salute.

After saying: "Each and every order of His Highness will be executed to the letter," he walked to the door.

Today his back was almost bent in two, but his head still wore its air of greatness. The second chamberlain went as far as the door. After saying: "You will designate the detectives you have seen fit to promote," he placed his hand on Pasha's sunken shoulders. Again in his eyes and his voice there was a softness coming from within that resembled Vehbi Dede, as he said:

"Don't be too upset, Pasha. All of us are no different from shadows that pass one by one."

As Pasha left the palace, his haughty lips curled with great bitterness saying:

"I would like to see the chamberlain go to Sabiha and tell her also that her son is a shadow."

As the black horses of his carriage flew off wreathed in white dust from the roads like the long tail of a comet, he seemed to see his wife, and particularly a very childlike act of hers. Every evening, the woman would insert her white hand into her son's collar, would investigate whether his back was or was not damp, would insist he change his underwear and make him drink a glass of hot linden tea.

"Thank God you are a pasha's son. The others are going to Yemen and Fizan!"

"Where is Tevfik going?"

"Also to Damascus …"

Hilmi was relieved, as if a mill-stone had been lifted from on top of his chest. The things that they would endure there would make this wretched man forget that he was wronged on account of Hilmi, perhaps they would take Rabia . . . Rather quickly he asked:

"When are we departing?"

"I will send you tomorrow morning to the steam-boat in a small launch. I have given orders, they will clean your cabin this evening."

"In what steam-boat are we going?"

"The Lord of the Sea."

Hilmi blanched.

"If we even pass Kadiköy, the sea will get me, so how will we go on the Mediterranean in that broken-down hulk? My mother's heart will sink if she thought I would travel on the open sea in Autumn in that wreck."

"We can make no exception … And why don't you like The Lord of the Sea? For twenty years it has transported soldiers and exiles to Yemen!"

Hilmi did not answer, made preparations to go out of the room.

"I would like to see you before you go, Hilmi."

"Why is that necessary, Milord? Now you have given your orders. I'm going to go to the street to say good-bye to a few friends."

"You cannot go outside before you go straight to the steam-boat."

"Oh …Very well … It that's so, you will find me in the evening in my mother's room."

From where had this dignity suddenly come to this lisping, spineless boy?

"If you go without telling your mother, can I not explain?"

"I will not go without having her blessing!"

"In any event, you will need money."

Pasha turned, held out a huge red satin purse to his son. Hilmi's eyes, when they saw that huge purse held out to him, widened and he brought his trembling hands to his mouth to shut in the chatter that desired to fly out of his lips. This red purse … This was the blood-money of everything his father did for the state!

Perhaps for half a second, or perhaps more, the two litigants looked at one another as if frozen. Hilmi's eyes were still dilated, and a red color had covered their whites. But when he began to speak, his voice was calm. It was so calm that for the first time Selim Pasha did not notice that Himi lisped.

"Put the purse in your pocket. It is henceforth not possible for me to accept money from you. Father, son, this relationship has now been completely sundered.

Hilmi had renounced Selim Pasha as a father, with the tranquillity and finality of a judge rendering a judgment ... And for the first time from his heart Selim Pasha felt respect and approval for his son. When the youth turned his back and left, his face ash white and his lips trembling, he slowly pulled the door closed as if he was closing a coffin.

The red purse on which the old man was buring his fingers was left and remained in the middle of his room. It was as if he was astonished that this insult awoke not wrath and mutiny but chagrin and pain. But his mind wandered to something totally different. He was thinking about the storms that happened frequently in the Mediterranean in Autumn. He went to the window, he pushed out the pane. It was a bright and starry night . . . The sky was blueish purple, the air was sweet, scented with roses ...There was no breeze, not even enough to dry out a woman's handkerchief.

Chapter Twenty-seven

The blackness dispersed. The top of the city-scape was wrapped in a fog of pearly whiteness. Minarets, turrets, with a point or without, all the shapes were far off, rubbed out, like things seen in a dream. The leaden surface of the water was sound asleep. Istanbul seemed like a silver misted morning dream.

The Galata wharf ... A group of rowboats and small lighters beside the wharf. Oarsmen were toying with their oars, growing impatient as the black-cloaked men listened to the sounds of carriages in the distance.

Shortly afterwards, one by one a troop of closed carriages came and stopped. Black cloaked men opened the carriage doors, from their interiors came black burkaed women holding handbags, some with children, some without, a few old men and dervish sheiks. Those who got out of the carriages drew near to each other, their hands became full as they touched shoulder to shoulder, then empty, clinging to one another with their hands as they tried to give each other courage; a human mass of misery, they descended into the rowboats and lighters.

The footfalls on the wharf stopped. The boats spread out over the leaden waters as they set sail ... They made their way straight to the Lord of the Sea anchored in front. In the middle of the fleet of rowboats and lighters, in the biggest lighter, Rabia was sitting beside a young woman giving suck to a child. There was a nip in the air. The two of them together were wrapped in Vehbi Dede's cloak. Under the cloak, Rabia was listening to the "glug glug" of the infant as she swallowed the milk. Opposite her, an emaciated old man with a pointed white beard and a Tatar face opened his eyes as if awakened from a nightmare, and began to wail:

"They are exiling my grandson, the unbelievers, let them throw a fig-tree into their

197

fireplaces.[44]"

The child suckling under the cloak abandoned the teat. "Viyak, viyak, viyak . . ."

A boy behind the lighter was wailing like a wolf cub. "Fa ... fa ... I want my father."

Again everyone was silent. The white-bearded old man's chin quivered, his collapsed lips were shaking, the oarsmen pulled their oars . . . A leave-taking whose end never came . . .

At last the rowboats and lighters drew near one by one to the Lord of the Sea. Black robed, black burkaed figures from the shaking decks landed on the steamboat, pushing and shoving. The boys one by one like monkeys, the girls sobbing and snivling, wailing and weaping, clambered up.

At the head of the ladder stood a barefoot crewman with torn trouser legs and a tassel-less fez. A crewman that for ten years had carried soldiers and exiles to Yemen and Tripoli in the Lord of the Sea ...

He opened his mouth and swore. A long rhymed, orderly stream of swear-words! At the helpless and friendless troops upon troops of wives and children, women and old men driven out to the Lord of the Sea at day-break; at those who were scattered like chaff to the four corners of the universe, sons, husbands, fathers, brothers of the black burkaed mound of the mourning; at those who made their living by putting out hearths and destroying house and home, earning their money that way!

The shower of curses turned to years past, to the ancestors of merchants of tyranny, to the ancestors of the ancestors, and arrived finally at Father Adam. The shower of curses blew into the years to come. By way of families out of families of merchants of tyranny, it arrived

---

[44] This curse is also found in Puglia, in Mola di Bari, and has to do with the fact that fig tree wood burns fast without giving much heat.

at the tyrant who was really the very last to torture human beings.

Doubtless this curse monument concerned the Sultan and the great men around him. But the black-robed ones had received orders "not to go to the root of anything," they pretended not to hear.

On deck, the hubbub and tumult rose to the sky. Rabia was a little confused, watching the young girl with the child who had been her companion in the lighter meet her husband. He seemed to be a poor young civil servant ... A thin man with shabby clothes ... The white bearded man with the Tatar face who had woken the child in the boat, his wrinkled hands in the air was shouting as if raving:

"Let them throw a fig-tree into their fireplaces!"

A young medical student pulled the old man's hands down, and shouted into his deaf ear: "My lord, my father, they have excused us from the festival, and if not from the festival, from the anniversary of the coronation."

Now the crewman, the master of the famous curse, a broken clay jug in his hands, distributed water to the people, chucked the babies under the chin, joked with the old women. But where indeed was Tevfik in the midst of this uproar?

Finally Rabia's eye found him too. He was trying to amuse in his lap the child of a fat woman struggling to make room for her husband on the deck. When he saw Rabia, he ran with the child. The father and daughter embraced one another, screaming and crushing the child between themselves. The woman ran and snatched up her child.

Tevfik's beard had sprung up, his cheeks were sunken, he had black and blue marks around his eyes. Without leaving father and daughter time to talk, from the bridge the captain's voice rang out like a trumpet:

"Hurry up … Ten minutes more and to the boats!"

Rabia placed a round bundle knotted from a handkerchief on Tevfik's chest. This was last month's earnings from the shop. Then, she also made room for her father on the deck beside the husband of the enormous woman. Rakim put down the baskets he had sweated to carry.

"There are grape leaves, olives, cheese, cold cuts… Write to us when you get to Damascus."

"Am I really going to Damascus?"

He did not yet know where he was being exiled. Everyone in his own mind was strolling about nightmare images of the classic exile places, Yemen and Fizan.

That evening, Vehbi Dede had come to Rabia to bring her the news that her father was going to Damascus; and the whole night, the girl had busied both her mind and her hand with Tevfik's underwear and food. As soon as the white streaks of dawn became visible, she and Rakim put them into the carriage and brought them to the quay.

A small launch approached the steam boat. The captain's voice once more rang out like an assault trumpet:

"Come on, to the boats!"

The black-robed ones went on deck. Once more they pushed and made the black burkaed mass descend.

The infant at the teat again cried: "Viyak!" The small boy howled like a wolf cub, the old man ranted his imprecation, the girls sobbing and snivling, wailing and weaping. The human wave swelled up and washed over the deck. Again the mound of misery, shoulder to shoulder, back to back clambered down into the lighters.

On the deck, men like a living pyramid crowded over one another and brandished multicolored handkerchiefs from the lighters that were setting sail . . .

The waters had woken up. Under the oars, there were flurries and spashes by the side of the rowboats. The sun played with the sea, on one side purple islands in a tulip light, on the other the half-moon shape of Istanbul's harbor . . .

The boats made their way to Istanbul. The sound of the echo stopped. The black burkaed ones, their eyes half closed, their hands in the sky, read some very long things, and then turning their heads they blew right at the place where the Lord of the Sea was.

Rakim asked Dede: "He is also exiled to Damascus, Tevfik's friend . . ."

Rabia said: "And I will become a maid to Miss Dürnev."

Vehbi Dede turned his eyes to the sea.

In the blue water with golden light and white foam, a school of dolphins passed, rolling playing and jumping over one another's backs.

Rakim said: "Tevfik asked me for the Karagöz sets. Is he going to do the "shadow" play in the steam- boat?"

Very contemplatively, Vehbi Dede answered:

"The shadow like the man is a country, and O my son, the country can be moved!"

HERE ENDS THE FIRST PART

26197829R00114

Made in the USA
Middletown, DE
21 November 2015